Books by Helen Hecht

SIMPLE PLEASURES *(1986)*

CUISINE FOR ALL SEASONS *(1983)*

COLD CUISINE *(1981)*

GIFTS IN GOOD TASTE *(1979)*
(with Linda LaBate Mushlin)

SIMPLE PLEASURES

SIMPLE PLEASURES

Casual Cooking for All Occasions

HELEN HECHT

ATHENEUM
New York
1986

Library of Congress Cataloging-in-Publication Data

Hecht, Helen.
  Simple pleasures.

  Includes index.
  1. Cookery.   I. Title.
TX715.H3993   1986   641.5   85-48133
ISBN 0-689-11523-7

Published simultaneously in Canada by Collier Macmillan Canada, Inc.
Manufactured by Fairfield Graphics, Fairfield, Pennsylvania
Designed by Kathleen Carey
First Edition

This book is for my son,

Evan

Acknowledgments

I wish to thank the many friends and relatives who have helped me with this book: my editor, Judith Kern, and designer, Kathleen Carey, for their discriminating taste and judgment; my husband, Anthony Hecht, who has to eat all the experiments and remain good-humored; my mother, Helen D'Alessandro, and sister, Carol Franklin, who help me with everything; my butcher in Rochester, Fred Quetschenbach, for excellent advice and information; and for recipes, Vee Angle, Mary Claire Heldorfer, Lee Willie Jones, William L. MacDonald, Susan Picone, Jill Stallworthy, Charles Stanback and Sherry Dunn of Victoria Swann, Ltd., and U. T. Summers.

Contents

Introduction

Most of us enjoy browsing through cookbooks that offer the latest word in haute cuisine, dreaming of extraordinary dishes to delight and astonish our friends. Nothing is too extravagant or difficult to tackle; only the decisions weigh one down—shall we conclude with a soufflé au Grand Marnier or a mocha-hazelnut dacquoise, for example? Those of us who are the Walter Mittys of the kitchen usually concede, however, that we'll never actually get around to cooking anything so elaborate. Few have either the time or the nerve for complicated, disaster-prone preparations. Such feats are better left in the capable hands of great restaurant chefs, for that is the sort of thing they are meant to do. Here, to illustrate the point, is Jay Jacobs reporting for the October 1984 issue of *Gourmet* on a meal served at La Côte Basque:

". . . a dinner date was presented with her starter. A tiny boneless quail, stuffed with veal sweetbreads, goose liver, shallots, and wild mushrooms, baked in a golden, form-fitting puff pastry, and served in a shallow pool of *sauce périgourdine* inscribed with arabesques of beurre blanc. Like Lewis Carroll's walrus, the lady wept as she ate."

A promising beginning to a restaurant meal, but folly to attempt at home, where it would more likely be the hostess who wept as she ate. Better to reserve haute cuisine for dining out than to break your spirit over the vol-au-vent.

This cookbook, by contrast, is meant to be easy. You will not be required, or even requested, to make puff pastry, gallantines, elaborate cakes, or difficult sauces. The recipes here are "simple" in a variety of ways. Some are for informal, country fare, such as soup or stew dinners that have few components and can be made well in advance of serving, eliminating any last-minute pressure. While none of the procedures is complicated or difficult, some stews will take time to prepare. There is another kind of simplicity in recipes that are composed of plain, fresh ingredients quickly and simply cooked. Such food tends to be light, to make the most of seasonal produce and fresh fish and seafood, and is well suited to summer dining. Sauces are usually based on lemon juice, fresh herbs, and butter. Some of these recipes are speedy, last-minute preparations, whereas others are cold dishes that can be made several hours before serving.

The challenge is to achieve simplicity without being ordinary. A hamburger and green salad is, without doubt, a simple meal, but there is no particular impetus, other than hunger, to make it. A scientist with whom I am acquainted has his own formula for entertaining: "My wife and I choose recipes on an inverse ratio of impact to effort." Dishes need not be rich and elaborate to be interesting. One can transform a perfectly plain salmon fillet by the addition of a sauce of fresh mint and orange juice or put together an unrivaled barbecue sauce with ingredients that are likely to be in your cupboard. A meal can often become memorable by its cumulative effect, felicitous combinations that make the whole a little more than the sum of its parts. The simpler the components, the greater the challenge to combine them in imaginative ways that actually taste good, avoiding the prosaic on the one hand and the contrived on the other. Sometimes it is the occasion that makes a party successful. Few people would think of serving hotdogs to guests, but a hotdog cookout with corn on the cob, farm tomatoes, homemade potato salad, and a peach cobbler can be a memorable event.

In addition to the recipes in this book, I have included a number of miscellaneous tips and suggestions for cooking procedures that I have discovered over the years. They have simplified my own work in the kitchen and may be of some use to you. There are, in addition, timesaving menu suggestions, such as easy hors d'oeuvres and appetizers, quick pasta dishes, interesting ways of serving store-bought ice cream, quick homemade ice creams, and simple fruit desserts. Menus appear throughout the text to suggest ways of combining some of the recipes in this book.

Notes on Ingredients

CHIVES When these are not available, substitute the tender green inner tops of scallions.

DÜSSELDORF MUSTARD The best brand of Düsseldorf that I have found is Frenzel, imported from Germany. If it is not available, use Gulden's Spicy Brown Mustard, an American brand found in most supermarkets. Düsseldorf is a mild mustard, as opposed to Dijon, which is sharp, but in some recipes, they are interchangeable.

EGGS Recipes are based on USDA-graded large eggs.

FLOUR Use all-purpose flour, preferably unbleached.

GINGER STEM A few recipes call for preserved ginger stem. These are knobs of ginger that have been candied and preserved in a syrup. They are packed in bottles and available in gourmet departments or specialty shops. A brand to look for is Rich's.

LEMON OR LIME JUICE Always use fresh.

MAYONNAISE Unless homemade mayonnaise is specified, use a good-quality commercial mayonnaise, such as Hellman's, but nothing labeled "salad dressing."

MINT   When fresh mint is called for, it is best to use the common garden variety of peppermint. Many markets carry spearmint, which may be substituted with caution, as it may have a faintly bitter taste.

OLIVE OIL   Use a light, virgin olive oil; those from Lucca, Italy, are very good. Extra-virgin olive oils from both Tuscany and southern France are excellent, but expensive.

SALT   The amount of salt required is rarely specified in a recipe, as this is a matter of individual habit and taste. Salt should be added cautiously, and only after a recipe has been completed, unless you are making baked goods.

TOMATOES   When fresh tomatoes are specified, use only ripe, locally grown, vine-ripened tomatoes. When tomatoes are not in season, good-quality canned tomatoes can be used for soups, stews, and sauces.

ZEST   The aromatic rind of a citrus fruit. Use only the colored outer part of the rind, avoiding the bitter white pith.

NOTE: In the sample menus, recipes marked with an asterisk are included in the book.

SIMPLE PLEASURES

Appetizers

APPETIZER SOUPS

CHILLED CARROT AND PEACH SOUP

The peaches in this soup subtly complement the flavor of the carrots, but are not readily identifiable. The soup can be served warm, but I think the flavor is best when chilled.

1 pound carrots
1 ¾ cups chicken stock or canned broth
2 medium-size peaches (½ pound), peeled and sliced
½ cup heavy cream
A pinch of ground ginger

Scrape the carrots and cut them into 1-inch lengths. Put them in a saucepan with the chicken stock, cover tightly, and simmer until the carrots are tender. Drain the carrots and reserve the broth. Purée the carrots in a food processor with the peaches. Stir in the broth and cream and season with ground ginger. Chill before serving.

3 TO 4 SERVINGS

CHILLED CUCUMBER AND HONEYDEW SOUP

I've always felt that cucumbers and honeydew have an affinity for each other and was not surprised to learn that they are related botanically. The addition of honeydew to a cucumber soup creates a particularly cooling potion for a humid summer day.

> *2 tablespoons unsalted butter*
> *3 tablespoons flour*
> *1 ½ cups chicken stock or canned broth*
> *3 large cucumbers (2 ¼ to 2 ½ pounds)*
> *⅔ cup fresh mint leaves, loosely packed*
> *1 small honeydew melon*
> *Salt*

FOR THE GARNISH:

> *Sprigs of mint*

Melt the butter in a small saucepan and stir in the flour. Gradually add the chicken stock and cook, stirring, until the mixture comes to a boil and thickens. Remove from the heat.

Peel the cucumbers, cut off and discard the ends, and quarter them lengthwise. Discard the seeds. Chop the cucumber coarse and purée with the mint leaves in a food processor. Add the thickened stock and blend. Turn into a container, cover airtight, and refrigerate. About 2 hours before serving, scoop out the honeydew from its rind. Cut enough of the melon into small cubes to measure 2 ½ cups. Add to the soup and season to taste. Refrigerate until serving. Garnish each serving with a sprig of mint.

4 SERVINGS

If you have a small patch of yard and sunlight, it is easy to grow fresh mint. And since it is a perennial, it will return faithfully every year. Mint has a variety of culinary uses that go beyond iced tea. It can be substituted for fresh basil in many recipes. It adds a bright and interesting flavor to many salads, such as pasta, chicken, steak, seafood, or a simple green salad. It can be used to make an unusual and delicious canapé (page 21); or, when added to applesauce, a conserve for lamb or pork. Mint is best when eaten fresh. Its flavor changes when cooked. I like the ordinary peppermint variety best. Spearmint, which is often sold in supermarkets, can have a bitter taste, as does orange mint and some other varieties.

CHILLED SPINACH AND MINT SOUP

The flavor of mint combines well with spinach to create a cooling and delicious summer soup. I use peppermint (the variety that flourishes— in fact, invades—most backyards), as it has no trace of bitterness.

Three 10-ounce packages fresh spinach
2½ tablespoons unsalted butter
3½ tablespoons flour
4 cups chicken stock or canned broth
2 egg yolks
1⅓ cups sour cream
⅔ cup heavy cream
2 scant tablespoons lemon juice
⅓ cup minced fresh mint leaves

FOR THE GARNISH:

Sprigs of fresh mint or very thin lemon slices

Wash the spinach well, discarding any stems or wilted leaves. Cook, covered, in a large enameled pot in the water clinging to the leaves. Drain well in a colander, pressing out as much water as possible with the back of a wooden spoon. Purée in a food processor and reserve.

Melt the butter in a large saucepan and stir in the flour. Gradually add the chicken stock or broth, whisking until the mixture comes to a boil and thickens. Lower the heat and cook below a simmer for a few minutes. Stir a little hot broth into the egg yolks, then add the yolk mixture to the pan, whisking vigorously. Cook for 5 to 10 minutes to thicken slightly, stirring often. Do not let the soup boil or the eggs will curdle. Remove from the heat and let cool to room temperature. When cool, stir in the spinach. Add the sour cream, stirring with a wire whisk, and then the cream, lemon juice, and mint. Cover and refrigerate until ready to serve. Garnish each serving with a mint sprig or lemon slice.

7 CUPS, OR 6 TO 8 SERVINGS

Cook spinach in an enameled or stain-less-steel pan. Aluminum, iron, and al-loyed metals will impart a metallic taste.

Also use enamel or stainless steel when making a custard or egg sauce such as hollandaise, as base metals will turn the yolks a greenish color.

CREAM OF ARTICHOKE SOUP

This is a delicately flavored soup that goes particularly well with a fish or veal entrée.

2 tablespoons unsalted butter
⅓ cup chopped scallions (white part only)
1 large Idaho potato, peeled and sliced thin
One 10-ounce package frozen artichoke hearts, partially defrosted
A pinch of dried thyme
2½ cups chicken stock or canned broth
¾ cup heavy cream

Melt the butter in a large skillet. Add the scallions, potato, arti-chokes, and thyme. Sauté for a few minutes over low heat until the scallions are softened, but do not let the vegetables brown. Add the chicken broth, cover the pan tightly, and simmer gently for 10 to 15 minutes until the potato is cooked through. Purée the vegetables with a little of the broth in a food processor. Turn into a bowl and stir in the rest of the broth and the cream. Reheat before serving, or serve chilled.

4 SERVINGS

TOMATO, ORANGE, AND FENNEL SOUP

Tomato and orange soup has always been one of my favorites. In this variation, it is delicately flavored with fennel seed. The soup should be served chilled and is very refreshing on a warm day.

> *2½ pounds ripe farm tomatoes, chopped*
> *1 large garlic clove, peeled and minced*
> *2½ teaspoons fennel seeds*
> *1 cup chicken stock or canned broth*
> *¾ cup plus 1 tablespoon orange juice*

Put the tomatoes in a large skillet with the garlic and fennel seeds. Bring to a simmer, cook for 1 or 2 minutes, and then add the chicken broth. Cover the pan and simmer for 30 minutes, or until the tomatoes are soft. Strain through a food mill and let cool to room temperature. Stir in the orange juice and chill before serving.

4 SERVINGS

TORTELLINI IN BRODO

Commonly served as an appetizer in Italy, this is a light soup of chicken broth with little cheese- or meat-filled rings of pasta. The tortellini can be bought ready-made.

FOR THE BROTH:

> *8 chicken backs*
> *1 large carrot, scraped and chopped*
> *1 medium-size yellow onion, peeled and quartered*
> *1 celery stalk, chopped*
> *Several sprigs of fresh parsley*
> *10 cups water*
> *2 chicken bouillon cubes (optional)*
> *Salt*

> *Vegetable oil*
> *½ pound cheese-filled tortellini*
> *Fresh-grated Parmesan cheese*

Rinse the chicken backs and remove any loose fat. Put them in a large kettle with the carrot, onion, celery, parsley, and water. Cover and boil gently for 2 hours, or until the meat is falling off the bones. Uncover and either continue to boil until the broth has a good flavor, or add a couple of bouillon cubes. After the bouillon has dissolved, taste the broth and add salt if necessary. Let the soup cool to room temperature, then strain and refrigerate. (The recipe may be made ahead to this point.)

To serve: Remove the layer of fat that has hardened on the surface of the broth. Slowly reheat the soup. Bring a very large pot of water to a boil to cook the tortellini. Add salt, a little vegetable oil, and the pasta. Boil until tender but still firm. Drain the pasta in a colander and add it to the broth. Serve immediately and pass a bowl of Parmesan cheese at the table.

8 TO 10 SERVINGS

Do not use a carbon steel knife to chop basil or other fresh herbs, as it will darken them.

VICHYSSOISE WITH FRESH BASIL

An interesting variation on a summer favorite. Prepare the soup at least 8 hours before serving to allow the basil flavor to develop fully.

3 medium-large leeks
2 large potatoes (1 pound)
2 tablespoons unsalted butter
3¼ cups chicken stock or canned broth
1 cup heavy cream
½ cup minced fresh basil leaves
Salt

Trim off the roots and the green tops of the leeks. Wash the leeks carefully and slice crosswise about ½ inch thick. Peel and slice the potatoes ¼ inch thick. Melt the butter in a large skillet and sauté the vegetables for 5 to 10 minutes, being careful not to brown them. Add the chicken stock, cover the pan tightly, and simmer for about 15 minutes or until the vegetables are soft. Drain, reserving the liquid. Purée the vegetables in a food processor, adding the reserved liquid in a thin stream. Let cool to room temperature, stir in the cream and basil leaves, and add salt to taste. Cover airtight and refrigerate until serving.

NOTE: To make the classic vichyssoise, omit the basil and garnish each serving with a teaspoonful of minced fresh chives.

6 SERVINGS

It is difficult to store fresh basil for much more than a day, since the leaves quickly wilt and turn black. To keep it for just a few hours, put the stems in a glass of water and refrigerate. To keep it overnight, wrap the stems in a damp paper towel, put the basil into a very large plastic bag that will trap a lot of air, and close the bag tightly. The basil should be dry before it is put in the bag, and there should be plenty of room for it to spread out to keep the leaves from rotting.

OTHER APPETIZERS

ARTICHOKES WITH DILL MAYONNAISE

Artichokes, served either warm or at room temperature, are a lovely first course for a spring dinner. They can be marinated after cooking in a Caper Vinaigrette (see page 14), or accompanied by the homemade mayonnaise given below.

> *4 medium-size artichokes*
> *Salt*
> *2 tablespoons lemon juice*

FOR THE DILL MAYONNAISE:

> *1 egg yolk*
> *1 tablespoon lemon juice*
> *1 generous teaspoon Dijon mustard*
> *⅜ cup light olive oil⎱*
> *⅜ cup vegetable oil⎰ mixed*
> *Salt*
> *1 teaspoon snipped fresh dill or ¼ teaspoon dried dill weed*

Cut the top third off each artichoke, then snip the thorny tips off all the remaining leaves with a pair of kitchen shears. Cut off the stems level with the base. Wash well under running water. In an enameled or stainless-steel pot just large enough to hold the artichokes, bring 2½ quarts of water to a boil. Add salt, the lemon juice, and the artichokes. Cover and simmer for 25 minutes, or until the bases can be pierced easily. Let cool to lukewarm, separate the leaves at the center, and pull and scrape out the chokes. Serve either lukewarm or at room temperature. Just before serving, fill the cavities with the mayonnaise.

To make the Dill Mayonnaise: Combine the egg yolk, lemon juice, and mustard in a small mixing bowl. Beat continuously with an electric mixer or wire whisk as you add the olive and vegetable oils drop by drop. As the mixture starts to thicken, increase the flow of the oil to a thin stream. Stir in salt to taste and the dill.

NOTE: If you make the mayonnaise in a food processor or blender, it will be necessary to use 2 egg yolks.

4 SERVINGS

When making mayonnaise, put 1 cup of oil in a 2-cup measure, as it is easier to drip or pour it slowly when the vessel is only half full.

AVOCADOS WITH CAPER VINAIGRETTE

This can be served as a first course or as a side dish. It is quickly assembled and goes well with almost any entrée. The avocados, however, must be perfectly ripe; and since most stores sell underripe avocados, you will have to plan a few days ahead.

FOR THE VINAIGRETTE:

> *⅓ cup olive oil*
> *1 tablespoon white wine vinegar*
> *1 teaspoon Dijon mustard*
> *1 garlic clove, peeled and cut in half*
> *1 teaspoon capers*
>
> *2 large, ripe avocados*
> *Fresh-ground pepper*

Combine the olive oil, vinegar, mustard, and garlic and let stand at least an hour to allow time for the garlic to flavor the vinaigrette.

Before serving, whisk the vinaigrette until it is homogenized and creamy. Discard the garlic and add the capers. Cut the avocados in half lengthwise and discard the pits. Peel, or serve in the skin, as you prefer. Spoon the vinaigrette into the cavities and season with ground pepper.

4 SERVINGS

FRESH CRABMEAT IN LEMON VINAIGRETTE

---

1 pound backfin crabmeat
¼ cup olive oil
2 tablespoons lemon juice
1½ to 2 tablespoons minced fresh dill or ½ teaspoon
  dried dill weed
Salt
Fresh-ground pepper
6 slices Pepperidge Farm very-thin-sliced whole wheat
  bread

FOR THE GARNISH:

6 Boston lettuce leaves or sprigs of fresh parsley

Carefully pick over the crabmeat to remove any shells or carti-
lage. Mix the olive oil and lemon juice and combine with the
crabmeat. Add the dill and salt and pepper to taste. Cover and
refrigerate until you wish to serve.

To serve: Place a lettuce leaf on each of six appetizer dishes
and mound a portion of crabmeat on each, or place the crabmeat
directly on the plate and garnish around the edges with a few sprigs
of parsley. Lightly toast the bread and cut each slice in half diagonally. Place two toast triangles on each plate.

6 SERVINGS

MUSHROOMS ON GARLIC CROUTONS

FOR THE CROUTONS:

2 tablespoons unsalted butter
1 garlic clove, peeled and slightly crushed
4 to 6 half-inch-thick slices French or Italian bread

FOR THE MUSHROOMS:

2 tablespoons unsalted butter
1 pound mushrooms, cleaned and trimmed, large ones
  halved
Fresh-ground pepper
Lemon juice
1 tablespoon minced fresh parsley
Salt

To make the croutons: Melt the butter in a large skillet with the garlic. Add the bread and sauté over moderate heat until lightly browned on both sides. Remove from the pan and keep warm.

Remove the garlic clove from the pan and add 2 more tablespoons butter. Add the mushrooms and sauté over very high heat, stirring, until browned. Sprinkle with plenty of pepper; add a few squirts of lemon juice and the parsley. Season with salt and serve immediately on top of the croutons.

4 TO 6 SERVINGS

PARMESAN, MUSHROOM, AND CELERY SALAD

This is an Italian dish that I've had in Venice, usually served as an appetizer. It does equally well as a side dish, to accompany or follow the entrée. As in many Italian recipes, a few simple ingredients are combined to create an interesting mix of texture and flavor.

FOR THE VINAIGRETTE:

⅔ cup olive oil
3½ tablespoons lemon juice
1 garlic clove, peeled and halved

FOR THE SALAD:

½ pound mushrooms, cleaned, trimmed, and sliced
2 cups thin-sliced celery
¼ pound imported Parmesan cheese, in one piece
Fresh-ground pepper

Combine the ingredients for the vinaigrette at least an hour before serving to allow the garlic to flavor the mixture.

Combine the sliced mushrooms and celery in a salad bowl. With a large, sharp knife, slice the Parmesan as thin as possible into pieces 1 to 2 inches long. Add to the salad, along with plenty of pepper. Discard the garlic clove and toss the salad with the vinaigrette just before serving.

6 SERVINGS

> *Mushrooms that are very dirty can be cleaned easily with a soft-bristled nylon brush. A soft toothbrush works as well as a mushroom brush and is less expensive.*

ROMAN-STYLE MELON

The ancient Romans ate melon dressed with a mixture of honey, lemon juice, pepper, and herbs—a preparation that makes a refreshing appetizer or a novel side dish. It is particularly good with pork, chicken, or a spicy stew.

½ medium-size honeydew, canary, or cantaloupe melon
3 tablespoons honey
2 tablespoons lemon juice
1½ teaspoons minced fresh mint leaves or ¼ teaspoon dried
⅛ teaspoon dried tarragon
Fresh-ground pepper

Remove the seeds and rind from the melon and cut into slices about ½ inch thick, allowing two or three slices to a serving. Combine the honey, lemon juice, mint, and tarragon and drizzle over the melon slices just before serving. Sprinkle with pepper.

4 TO 6 SERVINGS

TORTELLINI WITH FRESH BASIL

This is an example of how good the most minimal preparation can be. Tortellini—small, filled pasta—can be bought fresh at pasta stores or dried in boxes. In this recipe, they are cooked and tossed with a fine, fruity olive oil and fresh basil, creating a wonderfully fragrant appetizer or a light lunch or supper dish.

Vegetable oil
½ pound tortellini, filled with cheese, spinach, or veal
1 small garlic clove, peeled
⅓ cup light, fruity olive oil
1 cup torn or chopped fresh basil leaves
Fresh-ground pepper

Bring a very large pot of water to a boil; add salt, a little vegetable oil, and the tortellini. Cook until tender, but not too soft. Drain well in a colander.

Grate a little of the garlic into the olive oil, and toss the oil with the pasta while it is hot. Let cool slightly before adding the basil (so that it won't wilt). Season with pepper. Serve either warm or at room temperature.

3 TO 4 APPETIZER SERVINGS

A CHECKLIST OF QUICK HORS D'OEUVRES AND EASY APPETIZERS

Unless you are planning a cocktail party with no dinner menu to follow, what to serve with drinks should not be a matter of concern. While it is a good idea to offer something with alcoholic beverages, it should be sparing and light, as the host's time and the guests' appetites are best reserved for the dinner itself. I keep, for my own reference, a list of simple cocktail snacks that require little preparation or none at all. That list follows, as well as a list of easy appetizers to fall back on when you want to serve a first course but haven't the time to prepare it. These suggestions are offered simply as reminders; the recipes themselves are self-explanatory and, indeed, familiar territory in many cases.

Quick Hors d'Oeuvres

Blanched or natural almonds or pecans, lightly toasted.

Raw pecan halves sandwiched with cream cheese.

Imported olives.

Spears of Belgian endive or cucumber slices spread with a soft cheese, such as Rondolé.

Rounds of very-thin-sliced whole wheat bread spread with mayonnaise and topped with either sliced cucumbers or cherry tomatoes. (Drain the cucumber slices between two sheets of paper towels so that they won't be watery.)

Small cubes of melon wrapped with prosciutto and speared with toothpicks.

Thin rounds of French bread topped with Brie or Cheddar and broiled until the cheese melts.

Mint canapés. (Mix ¾ cup minced fresh mint leaves with ⅓ cup mayonnaise. Cut rounds of very-thin-sliced white bread, spread with a thin layer of mayonnaise, and top with the mint mixture.)

Spoonfuls of a soft, mild chèvre wrapped in prosciutto and secured with toothpicks.

Cocktail-size hotdogs or sausages broiled until brown and served with a pot of Dijon mustard.

Small triangles of paper-thin Marouk bread (Middle Eastern flat bread); buttered; sprinkled with dill, Parmesan, or sesame seeds; and lightly toasted under the broiler.

Squares of thin pumpernickel bread spread with sour cream or cream cheese and topped with smoked salmon.

Cherry tomatoes stuffed with a mixture of cottage cheese and minced fresh basil or chives.

Following are two hors d'oeuvre recipes that require fuller instructions.

COCKTAIL PECANS

½ pound (2 generous cups) shelled pecans
2 tablespoons unsalted butter
1 teaspoon Worcestershire sauce
Salt

Preheat the oven to 350°. Put the pecans in a large baking pan. Melt the butter with the Worcestershire sauce and drizzle it over the pecans. Stir to coat the nuts and spread them evenly in a single layer. Bake for 5 minutes. Drain on paper towels and salt lightly.

2 CUPS

LACY CHEDDAR WAFERS

These appear to be crisp, lacy cookies but are, in fact, simply melted cheese. They look lovely, taste good, and are a cinch to make, provided you have a Teflon or other nonstick baking sheet, as they will stick to any other surface, even if lined and well-buttered.

Preheat the oven to 350°. Cut slices of sharp Cheddar cheese about ¼ inch thick and 1 inch square. Place at least 2 inches apart on a nonstick baking sheet and bake for 8 to 10 minutes, or until lacy. Let cool for a minute and then remove with a spatula and transfer to paper towels to drain. (Note that as they bake, the wafers may slide toward the sides of the pan and stick together. If they do, break them into smaller pieces when they are cool.)

Easy Appetizers

Paper-thin slices of prosciutto with sliced melon, pears, or fresh figs.

Alternating slices of tomato and either fresh mozzarella or chèvre cheese, drizzled with olive oil and fresh basil.

Smoked salmon with capers and lemon wedges.

Smoked trout with horseradish–sour-cream sauce.

Crosse and Blackwell jellied madrilène garnished with lemon wedges and/or sour cream and chives.

Asparagus or leeks vinaigrette.

Shrimp and sliced avocado in curried Russian dressing.

Mixed antipasto, such as salami, imported olives, goat cheese, marinated mushrooms, tuna, hard-boiled eggs, capers, fennel, etc.

See also:
Avocados with Caper Vinaigrette, page 14.
Fresh Crabmeat in Lemon Vinaigrette, page 15.
Parmesan, Mushroom, and Celery Salad, page 17.
Roman-Style Melon, page 18.

Entrée Soups & Stews

THE entrées in this section are unpretentious country fare, essentially one-pot meals that need little more than rice or bread and a salad to complete the menu. Many are intended as soup suppers—light kitchen or fireside meals—whereas others are hearty stews ideal for informal entertaining. Although the stews may take a little extra time to prepare, they are practical dishes to serve when coping with a number of guests, since they can be made a day or two in advance, relieving you of last-minute pressure.

Suggested Menu

*BEEF STEW WITH APPLES AND GINGER

*LEMON RICE

GREEN SALAD

*MARRONS ICE CREAM

BEEF STEW WITH APPLES AND GINGER

3 pounds lean stewing beef,
  cut into 1-inch cubes
3 tablespoons vegetable oil
3 large garlic cloves, peeled
  and minced
3 medium-size celery stalks,
  chopped fine
2 cups chopped yellow
  onions
3 tablespoons minced
  fresh parsley
¼ cup flour

4 cups beef stock or
  canned bouillon
1 cup apple cider
1½ tablespoons fine-
  diced peeled fresh
  gingerroot
⅔ cup applejack
⅓ cup dried currants
2 small tart, crisp apples,
  such as McIntosh or
  Empire

Dry the beef well with paper towels. Heat the oil in a large skillet (not enameled) and brown the beef on all sides over moderately high heat. Do this in several batches so that the pan is not crowded. As the meat is browned, transfer it to a heavy casserole or Dutch oven.

Add more oil to the skillet if necessary and sauté the garlic, celery, and onions over low heat until soft but not brown. Stir in the parsley, then add the flour, stirring to blend. Add the vegetables to the casserole with the beef. Deglaze the skillet with a little of the beef stock, then pour it into the casserole with the remaining stock, the cider, gingerroot, and ⅓ cup of the applejack. Cover and simmer gently for 1½ to 2 hours, or until the meat is tender. Meanwhile, put the currants and remaining applejack in a small saucepan; cover and simmer until the liquid is absorbed, then add this to the stew. (The recipe may be made ahead to this point.)

To serve: Reheat the stew. Peel, core, and slice the apples into wedges about ¼ inch thick. Add to the stew and simmer 1 or 2 minutes longer, but do not let the apples get soft. Serve immediately.

6 SERVINGS

Store fresh gingerroot in the freezer. It can be grated or sliced more easily when frozen, and it will keep indefinitely.

To slice or chop an onion, cut it in half and place the cut side down on the chopping board so that it can be held steady.

BEEF STEW WITH ORANGE AND CUMIN

Vegetable oil
3 pounds lean stewing beef
  cut into 1-inch cubes
2 cups chopped
  yellow onions
2 garlic cloves, peeled and
  minced
1 medium-size sweet red
  pepper, seeded and
  chopped
Two 16-ounce cans
  tomatoes, drained,
  seeded, and chopped

2½ cups beef stock or
  canned bouillon
⅔ cup dry red wine
1¼ cups orange juice
½ teaspoon dried
  thyme
½ teaspoon dried basil
1½ teaspoons ground
  cumin
½ teaspoon ground
  coriander

Heat a film of vegetable oil in a large skillet. Dry the beef with paper towels and brown it on all sides, in several batches, over moderately high heat. As it is browned, transfer to a heavy casserole. Wipe out the pan if there is a burned residue on the bottom and add more oil. Sauté the onions, garlic, and red pepper until softened, but not brown. Transfer to the casserole with the beef and add the remaining ingredients. Cover and simmer gently on top of the stove for 1 hour, then continue cooking, partially covered, for 30 to 45 minutes, or until the meat is tender. Skim off any fat before serving, but do not thicken with flour or cornstarch, as it would mute and obscure the clear, bright flavor of the broth.

6 SERVINGS

Suggested Menu

*BLACK BEAN SOUP

ASSORTED GARNISHES

FRENCH BREAD AND CHEDDAR CHEESE

*SPINACH, AVOCADO, AND
RED PEPPER SALAD

FRESH FRUIT

BLACK BEAN SOUP

---

*1 pound (2 cups) black
    beans*
9 cups cold water
*3 tablespoons unsalted
    butter*
*2 cups fine-chopped yellow
    onions*
1 celery stalk, chopped fine
*2 large garlic cloves,
    peeled and minced*

*2 tablespoons minced
    fresh parsley*
1 bay leaf
*1 smoked pork hock
    (10 to 12 ounces)*
*3 cups chicken stock
    or canned broth*
*2 tablespoons lemon
    juice*
¼ cup Madeira
Fresh-ground pepper

FOR THE GARNISH:

Lemon slices
Chopped hard-boiled egg
Minced fresh chives
Sour cream

Soak the beans overnight in 8 cups of the water.

In a large heavy saucepan or Dutch oven, melt the butter and sauté the onions, celery, and garlic until soft but not brown. Add the parsley, bay leaf, and pork hock. Pour in the beans and their soaking liquid, the remaining 1 cup water, and the chicken stock. Partially cover, bring to a simmer, and cook gently for 3 to 3½ hours, or until the beans are very soft. Remove the pork hock and the bay leaf, and purée the soup through a food mill. Add the lemon juice, Madeira, and pepper. (The soup may be made ahead to this point.)

To serve: Reheat the soup, thinning if necessary with a little water or broth. Taste, and adjust the flavorings, adding more lemon juice or Madeira if you like. Serve with a lemon slice in each bowl and put the chopped egg, chives, and sour cream in separate bowls on the table.

4 ENTRÉE SERVINGS

Hard-boiled eggs can be peeled more easily if cooled first under cold running water.

Suggested Menu

*CHILI

*EASY CHEDDAR BREAD

*SLICED AVOCADO AND CANTALOUPE

*ORANGE ICE CREAM

*MARY CLAIRE'S OATMEAL COOKIES

CHILI

Chili is one of those dishes that make winter tolerable—just the sort of meal for informal fireside entertaining. The version below is made without beans.

1 sweet green bell or Cuban pepper, seeded and chopped
1 large sweet red pepper, seeded and chopped
Olive oil
4 cups chopped yellow onion
4 to 5 large garlic cloves, peeled and minced
3 pounds lean ground beef (round or lean chuck)
Two 28-ounce cans Italian tomatoes, packed in purée
1 cup tomato purée

3 cups beef stock or canned broth
⅔ cup beer
2 teaspoons ground cumin
1 teaspoon sweet paprika
3 to 4 tablespoons chili powder
Dried hot red pepper flakes
12 ounces shredded Cheddar cheese

Sauté the peppers in a large skillet in 2 tablespoons olive oil for about 10 minutes; do not brown. Add the onion, garlic, and a little more oil if necessary, and sauté without browning until the vegetables are very soft. Remove from the pan and reserve.

Add more oil if the skillet seems dry, and brown the beef in batches over moderately high heat for a few minutes, breaking it up with a fork. Transfer the beef and vegetables to a heavy casserole and add the tomatoes and the purée in which they were packed. With a metal spoon, cut the tomatoes into large pieces. Add an additional cup of tomato purée, the beef stock, beer, cumin, paprika, chili powder, and hot red pepper flakes to taste. Simmer gently, uncovered, for about 1½ hours. Taste, and adjust seasoning. (The recipe may be made ahead to this point.)

To serve: Reheat the chili and ladle it into deep flameproof soup bowls. Cover with a layer of shredded cheese and place under the broiler (about 9 inches below, if the shelf is adjustable). Broil just until the cheese melts, about 1 minute. If you don't have flameproof bowls, simply pass the cheese at the table.

6 SERVINGS

When making a soup, stew, sauce, or other prepared dish, do not add salt until the cooking is completed. Many recipes boil down, becoming saltier as they cook, and many include ingredients, such as canned broth, that are already quite salty.

Suggested Menu

*CIOPPINO

*HERB AND PARMESAN BREAD

GREEN SALAD WITH ARUGOLA

*ORANGE ICE CREAM

*CREAMY CHOCOLATE BROWNIES

CIOPPINO

This is a particularly hearty fish stew, made with tomatoes and red wine, which seem well suited to the robust flavors of the shellfish. The preparation is simplified because it is not necessary to make a separate fish stock. The recipe comes from a friend, Susan Picone.

1 generous cup chopped
   yellow onions
3 large garlic cloves, peeled
   and minced
3 tablespoons minced fresh
   parsley
2 tablespoons olive oil
Three 14½-ounce cans
   Italian plum tomatoes,
   packed in juice
One 16-ounce can tomato
   purée
1 cup dry red wine
½ cup water
2 to 3 teaspoons red
   wine vinegar
1 teaspoon dried basil

¼ teaspoon dried
   rosemary
⅛ teaspoon dried
   tarragon
⅛ to ¼ teaspoon
   saffron
A pinch of hot red
   pepper flakes, or
   to taste
1 large lobster (2½
   pounds)
1½ pounds sea scallops
½ pound large shrimp,
   shelled and deveined
2 dozen mussels, well
   scrubbed and beards
   removed

In a large, heavy casserole, gently sauté the onions, garlic, and parsley in the olive oil; do not brown. Drain the tomatoes, reserving the juice. Cut them in halves or quarters and drain them again in a colander. Add the tomatoes, tomato purée, wine, water, vinegar, herbs, saffron, and pepper flakes to the casserole. Bring to a boil, lower the heat, and simmer very gently, uncovered, for 40 to 45 minutes. (The recipe may be made ahead to this point.)

Kill the lobster by plunging a knife between the body and tail, or ask the fishmonger to do this if you buy the lobster shortly before cooking it. Working over a pan to collect any juices, pull off the tail, in its shell, and cut it into three or four pieces. Cut off and crack the claws. Cut the body lengthwise into two pieces. If it is a hen lobster, reserve the coral. Discard the intestinal sac and liver.

To cook, reheat the sauce, adding a little of the reserved tomato juice if the sauce seems too thick. Stir in the lobster pieces and any lobster juice and coral. Cover the pan tightly and simmer gently for 5 minutes. Add the scallops, shrimp, and mussels and simmer, covered, for 15 to 20 minutes longer, or until the mussels open wide. (Be sure the liquid is simmering and not boiling or the sauce may burn and the shellfish will cook much faster.) Discard any mussels that do not open.

Serve in large, heated soup plates, accompanied by warm Herb and Parmesan Bread (page 198). Put an empty bowl on the table for the shells.

4 SERVINGS

To store parsley, put the stems in a glass of water, cover the leafy portion with a plastic bag, and keep in the refrigerator.

FISH CHOWDER

This simple, old-fashioned soup makes a good family supper.

2 ounces salt pork or 2 slices
   bacon, diced
1 large celery stalk, diced
3 to 4 leeks, peeled, sliced,
   and washed well
1 tablespoon unsalted butter
3 medium-size potatoes,
   peeled and sliced ¼
   inch thick
2 cups chicken stock or
   canned broth or fish stock
½ teaspoon dried marjoram
2 tablespoons minced
   fresh parsley

1¼ pounds cod or
   scrod fillets, cut into
   large pieces
1½ cups half and half
   or light cream
½ pound bay scallops
½ teaspoon
   Worcestershire sauce
Salt
Fresh-ground pepper
1 tablespoon minced
   chives or green
   scallion ends

In a Dutch oven or large, heavy saucepan, fry the salt pork or bacon until crisp. Add the celery and cook for 5 minutes. Add the leeks and butter and sauté over moderate heat until the vegetables are soft but not brown. Add the potatoes, stock, marjoram, and parsley, and simmer, partially covered, for 10 minutes. Add the cod and cook 5 to 10 minutes longer. Add the half and half, scallops, and Worcestershire sauce and slowly return to a simmer. Remove from the heat, season with salt and pepper, sprinkle with the chives, and serve.

4 SERVINGS

FISH GUMBO

This recipe comes from Charles Stanback, a splendid cook and the owner of a superb butcher and catering business called Victoria Swann, Ltd., which he runs at Charles Foods in Washington, D.C. He often sells this soup in the shop, and whenever I see it there, I bring it home for dinner. It is a meal in itself, hearty and delicious. All you need to serve with it is plenty of garlic bread and a green salad. Natural gelatin from the fish bones replaces the okra in this recipe, giving the gumbo its characteristic viscous quality.

3 pounds whole bottom fish, such as flounder, perch, sole, turbot

4 quarts water

3 tablespoons Old Bay seafood seasoning*

1 pound crab legs

1 pound scallops

1 pound shrimp, shelled and deveined

One 28-ounce can tomatoes, drained, or 1¼ pounds fresh tomatoes, peeled and chopped

1⅔ cups chopped yellow onions

½ cup chopped scallions

1 medium-size sweet green pepper, seeded and chopped fine

28 ounces Hunt's tomato paste†

¼ cup brown sugar, lightly packed

One 6-ounce can small pitted black olives, drained (optional)

---

* Old Bay is a spice mixture that includes celery salt, dry mustard, pepper, bay leaves, and pimiento. If it is not available, substitute a similar mixture.

† If you substitute Contadina tomato paste, or an imported brand, use only 20 ounces, as it is more concentrated.

Prepare a fish stock: Put the whole fish into a very large stockpot, add the water and seafood seasoning, cover tightly, and simmer for 2 hours. Strain the stock and reserve.

Remove the fish meat from the skeletons, being careful to discard any small bones, and add the fish to the stock. Cut the crab legs at the joints and add to the stock with the scallops, shrimp, and tomatoes. (If you are using canned tomatoes, break them up with a metal spoon.) Stir in the remaining ingredients, except the olives. Partially cover and cook over very low heat for 4 hours. (Note that the secret to making this soup successfully is in the long, slow cooking. The liquid must never boil; maintain the temperature at 140° to 160° so that the soup barely simmers.) Uncover and continue to cook over very low heat for 4 hours longer, stirring occasionally. If you are using the olives, add them during the last hour of cooking.

12 SERVINGS

Suggested Menu

*FISHERMAN'S STEW

*BACON-CORN BREAD

*SPINACH, AVOCADO, AND
RED PEPPER SALAD

*PEACH-BRANDY PIE

FISHERMAN'S STEW

This is a hearty American-style fish soup with a tomato base. Serve it with large garlic croutons or French bread.

2 slices bacon
2 celery stalks, chopped
1 sweet red pepper, seeded
   and cut into strips
2 cups chopped yellow
   onions
1 large garlic clove, peeled
   and minced
3 tablespoons minced fresh
   parsley
½ teaspoon dried marjoram
1½ teaspoons curry powder

One 28-ounce can
   tomatoes, packed
   in juice
1 cup tomato purée or
   Hunt's tomato sauce
2 teaspoons
   Worcestershire sauce
A large pinch of hot
   red pepper flakes
1¼ pounds scrod or
   other thick, firm,
   non-oily fish fillets
1 pound mussels

Broil or fry the bacon, reserving the fat. Drain on paper towels and crumble. In a large casserole or Dutch oven, sauté the celery, red pepper, onion, and garlic in 2 tablespoons of the bacon fat until soft. Stir in the herbs, curry powder, the tomatoes and the juice in which they were packed, the tomato purée or sauce, Worcestershire sauce, pepper flakes, and bacon. Use a metal spoon to break up the tomatoes into halves or quarters. Cover and simmer for 10 minutes.

Meanwhile, cut the fish fillets into 1½-inch pieces. Scrub the mussels carefully under running water and remove their beards. Add the scrod and mussels to the stew and cook, covered, for 5 to 10 minutes, or just until the mussels open wide. If any fail to open, discard them before serving.

4 SERVINGS

Suggested Menu

*MINESTRONE

WHOLE WHEAT ITALIAN BREAD

CHEESE

FRESH FRUIT

MINESTRONE

1⅓ cups dried Great
  Northern white beans
4 cups sliced yellow onions
3 large garlic cloves, peeled
  and minced
5 tablespoons olive oil
1¼ pounds zucchini, sliced
  ¼ inch thick (4 cups)
1 pound fresh green beans,
  cut into ¾-inch lengths
3 to 4 celery stalks, sliced ¼
  inch thick
4 large carrots, scraped and
  sliced thin
1 medium-size head of
  escarole, washed, drained,
  and chopped coarse

5⅓ cups beef stock or
  canned broth
3½ cups chicken stock
  or canned broth
1½ pounds potatoes,
  peeled and cut into
  ¼-inch slices
1¼ pounds fresh
  tomatoes, peeled
  and chopped, or one
  28-ounce can
  tomatoes, drained
  and chopped
1½ teaspoons dried
  basil
Fresh-grated Parmesan
  cheese

Wash and pick over the white beans. Cover with water and either soak overnight or boil for 2 to 3 minutes and let stand, off the heat and covered, for 1 hour. Drain and reserve.

In a very large skillet, sauté the onions and garlic in 2 tablespoons of the oil until softened, but not brown. Add the zucchini, green beans, celery, carrots, and 2 more tablespoons of the oil and cook for 5 to 10 minutes over moderate heat, stirring occasionally. Add the escarole and the remaining tablespoon of oil and cook, stirring, until the escarole is wilted. Turn into a heavy casserole or Dutch oven and add the beef broth, chicken broth, potatoes, tomatoes, basil, and white beans. Partially cover, bring to a simmer, and cook very gently for 2½ to 3 hours, or until the beans are tender. If too much liquid boils away as the soup cooks, add a little water. Serve in large soup plates, and sprinkle each serving generously with Parmesan cheese. Serve warm French bread on the side.

NOTE: This recipe makes several quarts of soup, but it keeps for several days in the refrigerator and is just as good when reheated. It also freezes well.

ABOUT 4½ QUARTS OR 8 TO 10 ENTRÉE SERVINGS

If you are grating Parmesan cheese in quantity, store what you don't use immediately in an airtight jar in the freezer.

If you buy carrots with their green leafy tops still attached, break these off before storing the carrots to prevent the vegetable from becoming too soft.

Suggested Menu

*ONION AND MUSHROOM SOUP

*EASY SOUR CREAM BREAD

GREEN SALAD

*APPLE CRISP

ONION AND MUSHROOM SOUP

This is a French onion soup with the addition of sautéed mushrooms, which give a wonderful, rich flavor to the broth. Although most onion soups contain some wine or brandy, I like this soup best as it is—without any spirits or herbs.

> 5 tablespoons unsalted butter
> ¾ pound mushrooms, cleaned, trimmed, and sliced
>   ⅛ inch thick
> 1 tablespoon vegetable oil
> 2 large garlic cloves, peeled and minced
> 1½ pounds yellow onions, peeled and sliced thin
>   (4½ cups)
> 4 cups beef stock or canned bouillon
> Fresh-grated Parmesan or Gruyère cheese

In a very large skillet, heat 3 tablespoons of the butter to foaming. Add the mushrooms and sauté over high heat, stirring, to brown them. (Keep the heat high and do not crowd the skillet. If your pan is not large enough, cook the mushrooms in two batches.) When brown, transfer them to a large saucepan and reserve. Put the remaining 2 tablespoons butter and the vegetable oil in the skillet. Add the garlic and onions and sauté slowly over low heat until they are very soft and golden, but not brown. This will take at least an hour. Do not undercook them or the soup will have a bitter taste. Transfer the onions to the saucepan when they are cooked. Pour in the stock or bouillon. (The soup may be made ahead to this point.)

To serve: Simmer the soup, covered, until heated through. Taste to be sure the onions are completely soft. If they seem the least resistant, continue cooking until they have lost any suggestion of a crunchy texture. Ladle into soup bowls and sprinkle generously with grated Parmesan. Or, if you would like the surface of the soup encrusted with a layer of melted cheese, ladle into flameproof bowls, cover with a slice of toasted French bread and a thick layer of grated Gruyère or Parmesan cheese, and place under the broiler until melted.

NOTE: To make a plain onion soup, follow this recipe using 2 pounds of onions and omitting the mushrooms.

4 ENTRÉE SERVINGS

Most plastic bottles of vegetable oil have an inner seal of aluminum foil under the screw top. Do not remove the foil, but puncture it in 2 or 3 places with a metal skewer. The oil can then be sprinkled out; or, if the bottle is squeezed, poured in a thin stream.

Suggested Menu

*POTATO, LEEK, AND CABBAGE SOUP

*EASY SOUR CREAM BREAD

SLICED TOMATOES OR GREEN SALAD

FRESH PEARS

POTATO, LEEK, AND CABBAGE SOUP

This is a wonderfully satisfying, comforting cold-weather soup—good for Sunday night supper, particularly with a fresh-baked loaf of Easy Sour Cream Bread (page 192).

2 *large leeks*
1 *small onion*
3 *medium-size potatoes*
  (*1 pound total*)
3 *cups chopped cabbage*
3¼ *cups chicken stock*
  or canned broth

½ *cup heavy cream*
3 *tablespoons fresh-*
  grated Parmesan
  cheese
Fresh-ground pepper

Trim off the roots and the green ends of the leeks. Slit to within an inch of the root end and wash well under cold running water. Slice into ½-inch pieces. Peel and chop the onion. Peel the potatoes and cut them in half. Put the leeks, onion, potatoes, cabbage, and stock into a soup pot. Cover tightly and simmer until the vegetables are tender, about 30 minutes. Remove the potatoes with a slotted spoon, mash them, and reserve. (The recipe may be made ahead to this point.)

To serve, reheat the soup and whisk in the mashed potatoes, cream, and Parmesan. The soup should be thick, but if it seems too thick, thin it with a little extra broth or cream. Add pepper to taste. (You may want to pass a bowl of Parmesan at the table, but I prefer the soup as it is.)

3 ENTRÉE SERVINGS

Suggested Menu

*SAUERKRAUT, PORK, AND
MUSHROOM SOUP

RYE BREAD

ROMAINE AND RED ONION SALAD

*PEAR AND ALMOND CRUMBLE

SAUERKRAUT, PORK, AND MUSHROOM SOUP

This is a fine, hearty entrée for an informal winter meal.

4 tablespoons (½ stick)
unsalted butter
2 large garlic cloves, peeled
and minced
3 cups sliced yellow onions
1 pound mushrooms,
cleaned, trimmed, and
sliced
Fresh-ground pepper
2¼ to 2½ pounds pork loin
blades, trimmed of fat
4 cups water

4 cups chicken stock or
canned broth
2 pounds sauerkraut
(preferably packed
in cellophane bags)
1½ cups (12 ounces)
beer (not dark)
½ teaspoon caraway
seeds
¼ teaspoon dried thyme
1 bay leaf

Melt 2 tablespoons of the butter in a large skillet. Add the garlic and onions and cook over low heat until the onions are very soft and yellow, but not brown. Remove from the pan and reserve. Add the remaining butter and the mushrooms to the pan and sprinkle with pepper. Sauté over high heat, stirring, until the mushrooms are lightly browned and the moisture has evaporated. Remove from the skillet and reserve with the onions. Add the pork blades to the skillet and sauté over moderate heat to brown on both sides. Transfer the pork to a large enameled iron casserole. Add the water and stock, bring to a simmer, and cook on top of the stove, tightly covered, for 45 minutes. Remove from the heat.

When the pork is cool enough to handle, strip the meat from the bones and shred it. Return the shredded meat to the broth in

the casserole and discard the bones. Drain the sauerkraut, reserving
the liquid, and add the sauerkraut, reserved onions and mushrooms,
the beer, caraway seeds, thyme, and bay leaf to the soup. Simmer,
uncovered, for 30 minutes. Taste, and if a stronger flavor is desired,
add a little of the reserved sauerkraut liquid. Discard the bay leaf
before serving.

6 SERVINGS

SCALLOP, TOMATO, AND TORTELLINI SOUP

2 tablespoons minced shallot
1 garlic clove, peeled and
    minced
Unsalted butter
One 28-ounce can
    tomatoes*
2½ tablespoons minced
    fresh parsley
Salt
Vegetable oil
½ pound tortellini

1 pound bay scallops
2½ cups chicken stock,
    or canned broth, or
    homemade fish stock
⅓ cup dry white wine
2 teaspoons minced
    fresh basil or ¼
    teaspoon dried
Fresh-ground pepper
Fresh-grated Parmesan
    cheese

* When tomatoes are in season, substitute 1¼ pounds fresh tomatoes, peeled
and chopped. After adding them to the skillet, cook gently until they are soft.

In a large skillet, gently sauté the shallot and garlic in 1½ tablespoons butter until soft but not brown. Drain the tomatoes and

chop them coarse, scraping out the seeds as you do so. Add the chopped tomatoes to the skillet. Turn up the heat and cook, stirring, until most of the moisture evaporates. Stir in the minced parsley.

Bring a very large pot of water to a boil, add salt, a little vegetable oil, and the tortellini, and cook until tender. Drain in a colander, turn into a bowl, and toss with a lump of butter.

Add the scallops to the pan with the tomatoes and cook for just a few seconds. Transfer the mixture to a large saucepan and add the stock, wine, basil, pepper, and tortellini. Gradually bring the soup to a simmer. Remove from the heat and serve immediately. (Be careful not to let the scallops overcook or they will toughen.) Serve a bowl of grated Parmesan on the side.

4 ENTRÉE SERVINGS

Meat & Poultry Entrées

T H E meat and poultry entrées that follow are intended for a variety of occasions. Some, such as Choucroute Garnie, Veal Shanks Braised with Artichokes, or Butterflied Leg of Lamb served with Apple, Mint, and Ginger Conserve, are suitable for large dinner parties. Other recipes, such as Lemon Broilers with Basil or Chicken Scaloppine with Parsley Sauce, are quickly and easily made and ideal for impromptu entertaining for two to four people. And scattered throughout are a few barbecue recipes that are frankly informal fare, absolutely delicious, and not the best choice when the duke and duchess come to dine, unless they like ribs; in which case I urge you to try Lee Jones's recipe for Spareribs with Barbecue Sauce, the best I've had in this genre.

Suggested Menu

*MUSHROOMS ON GARLIC CROUTONS

*BUTTERFLIED LEG OF LAMB

*APPLE, MINT, AND GINGER CONSERVE

*CREAMED SPINACH

TOMATO AND RED ONION SALAD

*RASPBERRY-CASSIS FOOL

BUTTERFLIED LEG OF LAMB

This is a splendid and easy way to serve lamb. The boned and butterflied leg is marinated in an oil and lemon juice mixture, which is then used for basting and creates a delicious pan gravy. The lamb is also served with a conserve of applesauce flavored with mint and ginger.

FOR THE MARINADE:

½ cup lemon juice
½ cup olive oil
2 large garlic cloves, peeled and crushed
⅓ cup chopped fresh mint leaves
¼ teaspoon dried rosemary
Fresh-ground pepper

4 pounds boneless lamb, cut from the leg and butterflied
Apple, Mint, and Ginger Conserve (recipe follows)

Combine the ingredients for the marinade in a shallow glass or ceramic pan. Put in the lamb and turn it over to coat both sides. Loosely cover with wax paper, and refrigerate for 8 hours, or overnight, turning occasionally.

Preheat the broiler and adjust the shelf as close to the heating element as possible. Remove the lamb from the marinade and blot dry with paper towels. Reserve the marinade for basting. Place the meat on a rack in a roasting pan and broil very close to the heat for 7 to 10 minutes on each side, basting with the marinade after it begins to brown. When cooked, the meat should be well browned outside and rare inside. Put the lamb to rest on a warm platter and carefully skim the fat from the pan juices. Cut the lamb into thin slices and add the carving juices to the pan juices. Serve the juices in a small pitcher. Place the Apple, Mint, and Ginger Conserve in a bowl and pass both sauces at the table.

8 SERVINGS

APPLE, MINT, AND GINGER CONSERVE

An accompaniment to lamb or pork that is fresh-tasting, novel, and easily made.

2 cups chunky applesauce
¼ cup fine-diced preserved ginger stem
⅓ cup chopped fresh mint leaves

Combine the applesauce, ginger, and mint. Serve either slightly chilled or at room temperature.

APPROXIMATELY 2 CUPS

Suggested Menu

*ARTICHOKES WITH DILL MAYONNAISE

*CHICKEN SCALOPPINE WITH
PARSLEY SAUCE

*GREEN NOODLES WITH PARMESAN

ARUGOLA AND BIBB LETTUCE SALAD

*GINGER ICE CREAM

CHICKEN SCALOPPINE WITH PARSLEY SAUCE

Chicken breasts, cut into thin scallops, are flavored with lemon, garlic, butter, pine nuts, and parsley. It is a light and delicate dish, but care must be taken not to overcook the chicken, which should be moist and tender.

> *2 whole chicken breasts, split, skinned, and boned*
> *5 tablespoons unsalted butter*
> *1 large garlic clove, peeled and pressed*
> *2 tablespoons lemon juice*
> *Salt*
> *Fresh-ground pepper*
> *¼ cup pine nuts*
> *¾ cup minced fresh parsley*

Rinse the chicken and dry with paper towels. With a sharp carving knife, slice horizontally through each breast half to within a ½ inch of the opposite side. Open each piece flat so that you have four large, thin, butterflied pieces.

Heat 2 tablespoons of the butter in a very large skillet with the garlic and 1 tablespoon of the lemon juice. Take care not to let the garlic brown. Add the chicken pieces in a single layer. Sprinkle with salt and pepper and sauté over moderate heat for about 2 minutes on each side, or just until the chicken is no longer pink inside. Do not overcook, or it will be dry. Transfer to a heated serving dish and keep warm. Add the pine nuts to the pan and cook gently for about 1 minute. Remove from the heat and stir in the parsley, the remaining tablespoon lemon juice, and remaining butter. Stir all together just until the butter is creamy, then spoon equal portions of the sauce carefully on top of each chicken breast to cover the surface. Serve immediately.

4 SERVINGS

Always wash your hands and the kitchen counter after handling raw poultry. Poultry bacteria can contaminate other foods and cause food poisoning. For the same reason, you should not stuff poultry until just before it is to be cooked.

Suggested Menu

*CHICKEN WITH BARBECUE SAUCE

*BUTTERED CABBAGE OR *BAKED BEETS

*QUICK WALNUT BREAD

*QUICK PEACH ICE CREAM

CHICKEN WITH BARBECUE SAUCE

This is a good recipe to zip up chicken when you've grown tired of it and it seems either too ordinary or too bland. The recipe works best with small chickens, no larger than 2½ pounds.

FOR THE SAUCE:

> ¼ *cup wine vinegar or mild cider vinegar*
> ⅓ *cup ketchup*
> ⅓ *cup plus 1 tablespoon apricot jam*
> *1½ tablespoons soy sauce*
> ¼ *teaspoon Worcestershire sauce*
> 1T Dijon mustard
>
> One 2½-*pound broiling chicken, cut in half*
> 2 *tablespoons unsalted butter, melted*
> *Salt*
> *Fresh-ground pepper*

Combine the ingredients for the sauce and simmer gently for 10 to 15 minutes, or until slightly thickened. Strain the mixture, pressing the jam through the strainer with the back of a spoon. (This step is necessary, as the sauce will be too sour if the jam is not thoroughly blended.)

Rinse the chicken, removing any visible fat, and dry on paper towels.

Preheat the broiler. If possible, adjust the rack 9 inches below the heat. If the shelf cannot be adjusted, lower the heat so that the chicken will not char.

Brush the chicken all over with the melted butter, season with salt and pepper, and place it, skin side down, on a rack in a broiling pan. Broil for 10 minutes. Coat with about one-third of the sauce and cook 5 minutes longer. Turn skin side up and broil 15 minutes longer, or until cooked through, covering with the remaining sauce after the skin starts to brown.

2 GENEROUS SERVINGS

Prepared dishes can be kept warm for a short time in an oven that is heated to 150° and then turned off. Keep the food covered so that it does not dry out. Do not, however, put a roast in a warm oven or it will continue to cook. A whole roast will keep warm for 30 minutes if it is loosely covered with foil and kept in a draft-free place. Sliced meat should not be kept warm but should rather be served immediately.

Suggested Menu

*CHOUCROUTE GARNIE

RYE BREAD

*WATERCRESS AND MUSHROOM SALAD

*SAUTÉED APPLES OR PEARS

CHOUCROUTE GARNIE

This version of the classic Alsatian recipe uses spareribs, which become particularly succulent when braised with the sauerkraut, as well as knackwurst. Look for knackwurst that is made without garlic—they taste better and are more digestible. This is a good dish for cold and damp winter weather. Boiled potatoes are a traditional accompaniment, but the dish seems to me filling enough without them. Serve the Choucroute with a pot of imported mustard and follow with a salad and a light fruit dessert.

6 to 7 pounds spareribs
8 cups sliced yellow onions
4 large garlic cloves, peeled
and minced
Vegetable oil
8 pounds sauerkraut,
preferably packed in
cellophane bags
3 large crisp apples, such as
Greening, peeled, cored,
and sliced thin
2 teaspoons caraway seeds

2 bay leaves
3 or 4 cloves
14 juniper berries,
crushed
Fresh-ground pepper
3 cups dry white wine
7 cups chicken broth
12 knackwurst (2 to 3
pounds)
Düsseldorf or Dijon
mustard

Cut the spareribs into individual ribs and trim off as much fat as possible. Brown on all sides, in batches, in a large skillet over moderately high heat. Transfer to a platter and reserve. In the same pan, sauté the onions and garlic until very soft and yellow, adding a little oil if the pan seems dry.

Preheat the oven to 325°. Drain the sauerkraut well in a colander and rinse briefly under cold running water. Squeeze out as much liquid as possible with your hands. Transfer the sauerkraut to a heavy enameled casserole, separate the strands with a fork, and mix in the onions, garlic, apples, and caraway seeds. Tie the bay leaves, cloves, and juniper berries in a cheesecloth bag and add to the casserole, along with the pepper. Pour in the wine and chicken broth, cover the casserole, and place in the oven. Cook for 4 hours. (The recipe may be made ahead to this point.) Put the spareribs in the bottom of the casserole, cover them with the sauerkraut, re-cover the pan, and cook 1 hour longer. Add the knackwurst and continue cooking for 30 minutes.

Serve with Düsseldorf or Dijon mustard on the side.

10 TO 12 SERVINGS

Always warm the dinner plates when entertaining in cool weather. An efficient way to do this is in the dishwasher. Turn it to the dry cycle then turn it on. It will take 10 or 15 minutes to heat the plates.

Suggested Menu

*ROMAN-STYLE MELON

*DELMONICO STEAKS WITH MUSHROOM
AND PEPPERCORN SAUCE

*ROAST ONIONS

WATERCRESS

*MOCHA-ALMOND ICE CREAM

DELMONICO STEAKS WITH MUSHROOM AND PEPPERCORN SAUCE

For this recipe, the steaks are browned quickly and served with a highly flavored sauce that is easily made.

> 7 *tablespoons unsalted butter*
> ½ *pound mushrooms, cleaned, trimmed, and sliced*
> 4 *Delmonico steaks, each about 1¼ inches thick,*
>   *trimmed of fat*
> 1 *tablespoon brandy*
> 1 *tablespoon Marsala*
> 1 *tablespoon Düsseldorf mustard*
> 2 *teaspoons green peppercorns, crushed*

In a large skillet, heat 1 tablespoon of the butter to foaming. Add the mushrooms and sauté over high heat for 1 or 2 minutes to brown lightly. Do not let them get too soft. Remove from the skillet and reserve. Add another tablespoon of the butter to the pan and sauté the steaks over moderately high heat (3 to 4 minutes on each side for rare meat). Transfer to a platter and keep warm. Deglaze the pan with the brandy and Marsala. Stir in the mustard, then add the crushed peppercorns, mushrooms, and any steak juices that have accumulated on the platter. Remove the pan from the heat. Cut up the remaining 5 tablespoons butter and add to the pan. Stir briskly just until the sauce is creamy and homogenized. Do not let the butter get oily. Spoon the sauce over the steaks and serve immediately.

4 SERVINGS

Suggested Menu

*GAME HENS WITH FRESH THYME
AND LEMON

*TINY PEAS AND SUGAR SNAP PEAS

PITA TOAST TRIANGLES

BOSTON LETTUCE AND
WATERCRESS SALAD

*GINGER ICE CREAM

*CREAMY CHOCOLATE BROWNIES

GAME HENS WITH FRESH THYME AND LEMON

Fresh thyme and many other fresh herbs have become widely available during the past few years and serve as inspiration for light, simple, and flavorful preparations. In this recipe, the combination of thyme and lemon juice gives a bright flavor to roast hens.

2 small game hens (1 to 1¼ pounds each)
⅓ cup lemon juice
1 small bunch fresh thyme
3 tablespoons unsalted butter, softened
8 large shallot cloves, peeled
1 garlic clove, peeled and cut in half

FOR THE GARNISH:

Several sprigs of fresh thyme

Rinse the hens, removing any loose fat. Dry with paper towels and place in a shallow, nonmetallic pan, just large enough to hold them comfortably. Pour the lemon juice all over the hens and inside their cavities. Coarsely chop several sprigs of thyme (about 2 tablespoons) and scatter over and under the hens. Cover with wax paper and marinate in the refrigerator for several hours, or at room temperature for 2 hours, turning the hens in the marinade a few times.

Preheat the oven to 375°. Drain off and reserve the marinade. Strip thyme leaves from their stems to equal 1½ tablespoons and cream with 1½ tablespoons of the butter. Loosen the skin over the breast meat and spread this mixture underneath the skin of each bird. Butter a roasting pan and put in the hens, breast side up. Scatter the whole shallots around them. Melt the remaining butter in a small saucepan or stainless-steel measuring cup with the cut garlic clove. Roast the hens for about 1 hour, basting several times with the reserved marinade and the melted butter. (Use some thyme branches to brush the butter over the hens.) When done, the skin should be browned and the thigh juices should run clear. Serve the hens with the shallots and pour pan juices over each serving. Garnish with a few sprigs of fresh thyme.

2 SERVINGS

HAM BAKED WITH ORANGE

Ham is an easy entrée to prepare for any number of people, but if it is to be good, you must choose the right kind of ham. Heavily smoked country hams are suitable for hors d'oeuvres, but, to my taste, are too salty to eat as an entrée, no matter how long they are soaked or preboiled. Most hams available in supermarkets are labeled "water added," and these are not the best choice when you want to serve a baked ham. Their texture and flavor is altered when they are injected with water and chemicals. They lose their firm, grainy texture and become spongy and they also lose their characteristic smoky flavor. Most butchers stock hams that are not "water added" and will cut off an end piece of whatever weight you require. My own butcher favors Morrell's E-Z-Cut hams.

7½-pound end of precooked ham, with bone in
3 cups orange juice

FOR THE GLAZE:

⅓ cup light honey
2 tablespoons curaçao

Allow time before baking the ham to preboil and marinate it. Cut a small piece off the cut end and taste it. If it is too salty, put the ham in a very large pot, fill with cold water, and gradually bring to a simmer. Remove from the heat and pour off the water. Taste it again, and if it is still too salty, repeat this process, pouring off the water as soon as it reaches a boil.

Put the ham, cut side down, in a baking pan just large enough to hold it comfortably, and pour the orange juice over it. Let the ham marinate at room temperature for a few hours before baking it.

Preheat the oven to 350°. Cover the pan tightly with aluminum foil and bake the ham for 1 hour. Heat the honey and curaçao in a small saucepan or stainless-steel measuring cup. Remove the foil from the pan and spoon the honey mixture over the surface of the ham. Return to the oven for about 5 minutes to glaze. Carve the ham, spooning some of the pan juices over each serving, or serve the pan juices separately in a sauceboat.

8 TO 10 SERVINGS

Suggested Menu

*LEE JONES'S SPARERIBS WITH
BARBECUE SAUCE

*CORN MUFFINS

*POTATO SALAD

*TOMATO, PEACH, AND
RED ONION SALAD

*QUICK STRAWBERRY ICE CREAM

LEE JONES'S SPARERIBS WITH BARBECUE SAUCE

Cooked this way, the ribs are moist and tender, not greasy, and are coated with a delicious spicy sauce.

7 pounds lean baby spareribs

FOR THE SAUCE:

7 garlic cloves
½ cup lemon juice
¾ cup mild cider vinegar
  or wine vinegar
¾ cup light honey
1½ tablespoons brown
  sugar
¾ cup ketchup

1½ cups Hunt's
  tomato sauce or
  tomato purée
¾ cup water
1½ teaspoons yellow
  mustard
1½ teaspoons hot red
  pepper flakes
Cornstarch (optional)

Preheat the broiler.

Pull the transparent layer of skin off the underside of the ribs. Cut off as much fat as possible. Put the ribs in a single layer on the rack of a broiling pan and place the pan 7 to 9 inches below the heat. Broil the ribs for 25 to 30 minutes, turning them over halfway through cooking so that they brown on both sides. Transfer to a platter and pour all the fat out of the pan.

To make the sauce: Peel the garlic cloves and slice them crosswise in pieces about ⅛ inch thick. Put the garlic and all the remaining ingredients for the sauce, except the cornstarch, into a 3-quart saucepan. Slowly bring to a boil, stirring. Turn the heat low, cover the pan, and simmer for 45 minutes or until the sauce is quite syrupy. (The recipe may be made ahead to this point.)

To finish cooking: Preheat the oven to 350°. Cut the racks into individual ribs. Place them in a single layer in one large or two smaller baking pans and pour the sauce over them. Cover the pans with aluminum foil and bake for 45 to 50 minutes, or until the ribs are very tender. The sauce should have thickened in the baking process. But if it is not quite thick enough, transfer the ribs to a warm platter, dissolve a heaping teaspoon of cornstarch in a little cold water and stir into the sauce; then boil briefly to thicken. Spoon the sauce over the ribs and serve.

6 TO 7 SERVINGS

Honey, syrup, or molasses will pour easily out of a measuring cup if the cup has been coated first with oil.

Suggested Menu

*LEMON BROILERS WITH BASIL

*GREEN BEANS OR *CORN ON THE COB

*TOMATO SALAD PROVENÇALE

*BLUEBERRY COBBLER

LEMON BROILERS WITH BASIL

For this recipe, the chicken is marinated in lemon juice, broiled quickly, and served with a delicious, piquant lemon-basil sauce made from the pan juices. It is particularly good with fresh corn on the cob and summer tomatoes.

> *2 small chickens (2 to 2½ pounds each), split in half*
> *⅔ cup fresh lemon juice*
> *Salt*
> *Fresh-ground pepper*
> *4 tablespoons (½ stick) unsalted butter*
> *½ cup minced fresh basil*

Put the chickens in a large enameled roasting pan and pour the lemon juice over them. Marinate all day or for several hours in the refrigerator, turning the pieces occasionally.

Preheat the broiler, and adjust the oven rack so that the surface of the chicken will be 4 or 5 inches from the heating element. Leave the chickens in the roasting pan with the marinade and arrange them skin side down. Sprinkle with salt and pepper. Broil for 15 minutes. Turn the chickens skin side up, rub the skin with 1 tablespoon of the butter, and season lightly. Broil 10 to 15 minutes longer, or just until the skin is golden brown and the meat is cooked through, basting once or twice with the pan juices. Transfer the chicken to a warm platter. Pour the pan juices into a small saucepan and, off the heat, stir in the remaining 3 tablespoons butter, then add the minced basil. Pour into a sauceboat and serve at the table or spoon the lemon-basil sauce over each serving.

4 SERVINGS

Writing in the 1950s, Elizabeth David observed, "A grilled chicken is perhaps one of the nicest foods at any time; everybody likes it, it needs very little preparation, it is quickly cooked, and although expensive, there is nothing to be spent on extras, so it could be much less rare than it is." *

I had forgotten, until reading this, that chicken ever was expensive, having regarded it for so long as one of the few economical foods left. It is, however, just as good as it ever was. Whether grilled, broiled, roasted, or fried, it remains one of the true gastronomic "simple pleasures." Like every food that is served simply, quality and freshness are essential. Many supermarket chickens have very little flavor and are tough or watery. Of the widely distributed brands, Perdue is the most reliable. Some butchers stock "free-range" chickens, raised on real farms instead of in chicken factories, and I have found the chickens in kosher markets to be fresh and of excellent quality, although they do cost more.

* *Summer Cooking* (Penguin Books, Ltd., 1955).

PORK CHOPS WITH POTATOES, ONIONS, AND ROSEMARY

A hearty supper dish that needs only a green salad to accompany it and fruit, such as fresh pears, for dessert.

Olive oil
1 tablespoon butter
2⅓ cups sliced yellow onions
2 garlic cloves, peeled and minced
2 large potatoes

4 pork chops, cut about 1 inch thick
Flour
½ cup chicken broth
¼ teaspoon dried rosemary
Fresh-ground pepper

Put 1 or 2 tablespoons of the olive oil and the butter in a large skillet and cook the onions and garlic, without browning, until soft. Remove from the pan and reserve.

Peel and slice the potatoes ¼ inch thick. Add a film of olive oil to the pan and sauté the potatoes until tender over moderately high heat, turning to brown both sides. Add them to the onion mixture.

Lightly flour the pork chops. Add more oil if the pan seems dry and brown the chops on both sides. Lower the heat, return the potatoes and onions to the pan, and add the chicken broth, rosemary, and pepper. Cover tightly and simmer gently for about 20 minutes, or until the chops are tender. Serve the chops with the vegetables and pan juices.

2 TO 4 SERVINGS

Cooking Pork and Veal Roasts or Chops
These meats tend to dry out when roasted in an open pan. They are best cooked in a braising liquid and tightly covered either in the oven or on top of the stove. Plastic oven bags provide an excellent method for cooking a pork or veal roast. A marinade or wine can be put in the bag with the meat so that it is continually basted while cooking. The roast will brown through the bag and will be tender and succulent when cooked. Moreover, cleanup is easy, as the roasting pan will not need scouring.

Suggested Menu

*CHILLED SPINACH AND MINT SOUP

*RACK OF LAMB

CHUTNEY

WATERCRESS

*CRUSTY POTATOES OR *ROAST ONIONS

*CHOCOLATE CURAÇAO CAKE

RACK OF LAMB

A rack of lamb is so good that you don't need to do much to it except roast it quickly and make sure it is not overcooked. In this recipe I suggest a simple basting sauce; it is not essential, but gives a delicate flavor to the meat.

2 racks of lamb (4 pounds or 16 chops total)

FOR THE BASTING SAUCE:

¼ cup lemon juice
3 tablespoons orange juice
3 tablespoons olive oil
2 garlic cloves, peeled and pressed
¾ teaspoon dried mint

FOR THE GARNISH:

½ cup chopped fresh parsley
Watercress

Major Grey's chutney

Ask the butcher to remove the backbone and trim off all but ⅛ to ¼ inch of the surface fat from the lamb.

Mix the ingredients for the basting sauce. About 2 or 3 hours before cooking, brush the meat with some of the sauce and let it stand at room temperature.

Preheat the oven to 425°. Put the lamb in a shallow roasting pan and insert a meat thermometer horizontally through several of the chops. Roast for 30 to 45 minutes, basting occasionally with the remaining sauce. For rare meat, the thermometer will register 140°. Note that the three or four smaller chops at one end of each rack will cook more quickly. If you want the racks uniformly pink, cut off these smaller sections when they are cooked, transfer to a heated platter, and cover with foil. (Do not separate them yet into individual chops). The smaller chops will probably be cooked in 30 minutes. Return the thicker sections of the racks to the oven to cook 10 to 15 minutes longer. When all the meat is done, shave off the top layer of surface fat and firmly press the chopped parsley on top. Return to the oven for 1 minute only. Then cut the racks into individual chops and place two on each plate with a small bunch of watercress. (Reserve the remaining chops for second helpings.) Serve a bowl of chutney on the side.

6 SERVINGS

Store watercress in the refrigerator completely immersed in a bowl of water.

Suggested Menu

*ROAST CHICKEN WITH
LEMON-CREAM SAUCE

*BABY CARROTS BRAISED WITH
ORANGE AND GINGER

*POPOVERS OR *SCONES

*PECAN PIE OR *DEEP-DISH PEACH PIE

ROAST CHICKEN WITH LEMON-CREAM SAUCE

No cookbook of this sort would be complete without a recipe for roast chicken, one of the great, truly simple, culinary pleasures. In this recipe, the pan juices are poured over bunches of watercress, which makes a delicious vegetable accompaniment, and a Lemon-Cream Sauce is served with the chicken. You may, of course, sauce the chicken more simply with the clear pan juices.

> *One 3½-pound roasting chicken*
> *1 lemon*
> *Fresh herbs, such as tarragon or thyme (optional)*
> *1½ tablespoons unsalted butter, melted*
> *Salt*
> *Fresh-ground pepper*

FOR THE SAUCE:

> *1 tablespoon unsalted butter*
> *½ cup heavy cream*
> *1 teaspoon Dijon mustard*
> *Fresh-ground pepper*
> *1 egg yolk*
> *1 tablespoon lemon juice*
>
> *1 very large or 2 medium-size bunches of watercress*

Preheat the oven to 375°. Rinse and dry the chicken, removing any loose fat. Squeeze the lemon, reserve the juice, and rub the cut lemon inside the cavity of the chicken. If you like, you may stuff the bird with a few sprigs of fresh herbs. Truss the chicken, tying the legs together in front, and wrapping the string around the body to tie in back under the wings. Rub the melted butter all over the skin, and with additional butter, generously grease the roasting pan. Sprinkle the chicken with salt and pepper, and roast for 25 minutes on its side. Turn on the other side and roast 25 minutes longer. As the chicken is cooking, baste it with 2 tablespoons of the reserved lemon juice and the pan juices. Turn it breast side up and roast 10 to 15 minutes longer, or until the skin is browned and the thigh juices run clear.

To make the Lemon-Cream Sauce: About 10 minutes before the chicken is done, melt the butter in a small, heavy saucepan. Add the cream and boil for 3 minutes, stirring often, to thicken. Take the pan off the burner and stir in the mustard and pepper. Whisking vigorously, add the egg yolk. Return to very low heat and cook for a minute, stirring continuously. Remove from the heat, stir in the lemon juice, and transfer to a warm sauceboat.

Serve the chicken with a generous bunch of watercress on each plate. Drizzle the pan juices over the watercress and the carved chicken. Pass the Lemon-Cream Sauce separately.

4 SERVINGS

SHORT RIBS WITH BARBECUE SAUCE

Try to get the last three ribs on a roast, which are the thickest, and have the butcher trim off the top layer of fat and gristle. For this recipe the ribs are well browned under the broiler and then braised in a mildly spicy tomato and orange barbecue sauce.

> *4 to 5 thick short ribs (each 5 inches long), trimmed of*
> *fat and gristle*

FOR THE SAUCE:

> *1 cup tomato purée or Contadina tomato sauce*
>   *(not spaghetti sauce)*
> *½ cup orange juice*
> *1 large garlic clove, peeled and pressed*
> *1 tablespoon wine vinegar*
> *1 teaspoon Worcestershire sauce*
> *⅓ cup sweet orange marmalade*
> *½ teaspoon curry powder*

Preheat the broiler and put the ribs in a single layer in a small baking pan. Broil the ribs for 15 minutes, or until well browned. (Adjust the oven shelf or the degree of heat so that they brown without charring.) Transfer the ribs to a platter and discard the fat. Return the ribs to the baking pan and reserve.

To make the sauce: Combine all the ingredients in a heavy saucepan and cook, just at a simmer, for 30 minutes to thicken slightly. Pour the sauce over the ribs and cover the pan tightly with aluminum foil. Preheat the oven to 350° and bake for 1¼ hours, or until the ribs are very tender.

2 TO 4 SERVINGS

Suggested Menu

*VEAL SHANKS BRAISED WITH
ARTICHOKES

*ORANGE RICE

TOASTED PITA BREAD

GREEN SALAD WITH ARUGOLA

*LEMON-GLAZED ALMOND CAKE

VEAL SHANKS BRAISED WITH ARTICHOKES

This dish is prepared much like the Italian osso buco, except that fresh artichokes, which go particularly well with the veal, have been added. It is garnished with a mixture of parsley, lemon zest, and garlic known as gremolata. Osso buco is traditionally served with risotto Milanese, a delicious but rich and painstaking preparation. Orange Rice (page 164) is a lighter alternative and can be left to cook on its own. This veal dish is a good choice for a dinner party—it tastes wonderful, it is not ordinary, and it can be made the day before serving.

8 to 9 pounds veal shank,
*   cut 1½ inches thick**
Salt
Fresh-ground pepper
Flour
2 tablespoons unsalted
*   butter*
2 tablespoons olive oil
4½ cups fine-chopped
*   yellow onions*
4 large garlic cloves,
*   peeled and minced*
3 medium-size carrots,
*   diced fine*
Three 28-ounce cans
*   tomatoes, packed in*
*   juice*
Several sprigs of fresh
*   parsley*

2 bay leaves
A few sprigs of fresh
*   thyme, if available*
1¼ teaspoons dried
*   marjoram*
Three 3-inch strips
*   navel orange zest*
*   (no white pith)*
3 cups dry white wine
3 cups beef or veal
*   stock or canned*
*   beef bouillon*
6 or 7 medium-size
*   artichokes*
3 tablespoons flour
*   mixed with 3*
*   tablespoons softened*
*   butter (optional)*

* Ask your butcher to use hind shanks and choose meaty pieces with small center bones.

FOR THE GREMOLATA:

½ cup minced fresh parsley
Grated zest of 3 lemons
1 medium-size garlic clove, peeled and minced

Sprinkle the veal with salt and pepper and dredge in flour. Heat half the butter and half the olive oil in a large skillet and brown the shanks, in batches, on both sides over moderately high heat, adding more butter and oil as necessary. Remove from the skillet as they are browned, and reserve. Wipe out the pan if the flour has burned on the bottom. Put the onions, garlic, and carrots in the pan, adding a little olive oil if necessary. Cook over low heat without browning until the onions are very soft. Put the cooked vegetables in the bottom of a heavy, flameproof casserole and place the veal shanks on top. Drain the tomatoes and chop coarse, scraping out the seeds. Add them to the casserole. Add the herbs, orange zest, wine, and stock, cover tightly, and bring to a simmer on top of the stove. Cook very gently for about 30 minutes.

Meanwhile, prepare the artichokes: Trim off the stems, the top third of the leaves, and all the tough outer leaves. Quarter the artichokes and remove the chokes. Rinse well, pat dry, and add to the casserole. Continue cooking, covered and at a simmer, for 15 minutes. Place the lid ajar and cook about 45 minutes longer, or until the veal is very tender. While the meat is cooking, combine the ingredients for the gremolata and reserve.

Before serving, skim any fat off the surface of the stew. If the sauce does not seem thick enough, stir in all or part of the butter-flour mixture. Sprinkle a teaspoon of the gremolata over each portion and serve Orange Rice on the side.

NOTE: If the stew has been prepared ahead, return to room temperature and then reheat, covered, in a 350° oven for about 30 minutes.

10 TO 12 SERVINGS

If the peel of a lemon or other citrus fruit has been cut or grated, the fruit will keep longer if it is tightly wrapped in foil or plastic wrap. Or squeeze the juice and store it in the freezer.

Fish & Vegetarian Entrées

FISH and seafood deserve particular attention in this book, for they are best when prepared with restraint and simplicity. A fresh-caught trout that has been perfectly grilled needs only a lemon wedge to enhance its flavor. And it would be difficult to improve upon a whole boiled lobster served with a simple lemon-butter sauce—a far nobler treatment than rich preparations such as Newburg.

In the recipes that follow, careful consideration is given to cooking method in order to assure that the fish doesn't dry out. Sauces are light and delicate, favoring fresh herbs and lemon or lime juice.

Because soufflés, omelets, and pasta must also be counted among the pleasures of simple dining, the chapter concludes with suggestions for their preparation.

Suggested Menu

*BOILED LOBSTER

*LEMON-DILL BUTTER SAUCE

*CORN ON THE COB

*BUTTERMILK BISCUITS

SLICED TOMATOES WITH FRESH BASIL

*QUICK PEACH ICE CREAM

BOILED LOBSTER

If you live within reach of the New England coast, one of the great pleasures of summer is boiled lobster. Boiling is, in my opinion, the best way of cooking lobster, as the meat remains moist and succulent, while broiling tends to dry it out. An elaborately prepared lobster can never be as good as a plain boiled one, served with a simple melted butter sauce and lemon wedges.

Allow one 1¼-to-1½-pound lobster per serving. Rinse them well under running water. Bring a very large pot of water to a rolling boil. Add salt and the lobsters, cover the pot, and return to a boil. Cook for 10 to 12 minutes. Before serving, crack the claws to allow some of the liquid to drain off. Cut along the length of the body on the underside and remove the intestinal vein.

To make the butter sauce: For each serving, melt 2 tablespoons unsalted butter with 1 teaspoon lemon juice and a large pinch of dried dill weed. Serve each lobster with its own small cup of melted butter and a lemon wedge, along with nutcrackers for breaking the shell.

BROOK TROUT WITH DILL AND CAPER SAUCE

Fresh trout have a fine and delicate flavor and texture. They are simple to prepare (I do not believe in stuffing them with anything more than a few fresh herbs) and are a treat on any occasion. If you don't have fresh dill, substitute parsley.

> *8 brook or rainbow trout (10 to 12 ounces each), boned,*
> *with the head and tail left on*
> *1½ to 2 tablespoons lemon juice*
> *Several sprigs of fresh dill*
> *Approximately 2 tablespoons butter, melted*
> *½ cup dry white wine*

FOR THE SAUCE:

> *1½ sticks unsalted butter*
> *2 tablespoons lemon juice*
> *2 tablespoons capers, well drained*
> *3 tablespoons minced fresh dill*

FOR THE GARNISH:

> *Sprigs of dill or parsley*

Preheat the oven to 375°. Butter one or two baking pans large enough to hold the trout in a single layer. Rinse and dry the trout. Sprinkle the inside of each with a little lemon juice and lay several sprigs of fresh dill along the cavity. Brush the skin of the trout with the melted butter. Pour the wine into the baking pans. Bake, uncovered, for 20 to 25 minutes, or just until the trout are cooked through at the thickest part.

To make the sauce: While the trout are cooking, cut up the butter, put it in a saucepan with the lemon juice, capers, and dill, and whisk over very low heat until just melted and creamy. Do not overheat or the sauce will get thin and oily. Turn into a sauceboat.

Place the trout on individual dinner plates and garnish each plate with dill or parsley. Pass the sauce separately.

8 SERVINGS

PAN-FRIED TROUT

This is a good way to cook trout when you are serving just a few people. For each person allow one trout (8 to 12 ounces), cleaned and with the head left on. Rinse the fish, leave the outside damp, and dry the body cavity with paper towels. Rub the cavity with lemon juice and season lightly with salt and pepper. Dredge the trout in seasoned flour. Melt butter and olive oil in a large skillet, to a depth of ⅛ to ¼ inch. When the oil is hot, add the trout and cook over moderately high heat until well browned on both sides, squeezing a little lemon juice over them as they cook. They will require 4 or 5 minutes on each side. (Cut into one at the thickest part to make sure it is cooked through.) These are superb garnished simply with fresh parsley and lemon wedges, but if you prefer, you may serve a bowl of Dill Mayonnaise (see page 12) on the side. (I like this with the trout, although mayonnaise is usually reserved for cold fish.)

Never store fish or poultry airtight. Put it in a bowl, cover loosely with wax paper, and refrigerate.

Suggested Menu

*AVOCADOS WITH CAPER VINAIGRETTE

*SALMON FILLETS WITH
ORANGE-MINT SAUCE

*GREEN BEANS

PITA TOAST TRIANGLES

*QUICK RASPBERRY ICE CREAM

*VEE'S SHORTBREAD

SALMON FILLETS WITH ORANGE-MINT SAUCE

This is a lovely combination of flavors in an entrée that can be made quickly and easily.

3 pounds salmon fillets
½ cup plus 1 tablespoon orange juice
3 tablespoons lemon juice
1 stick plus 1 tablespoon unsalted butter
Fresh-ground pepper
1 cup chopped fresh mint leaves

Preheat the oven to 375°. Butter the bottom of a large baking dish. Rinse the salmon, pat dry with paper towels, and place in the pan in a single layer, skin side down. Pour the orange and lemon juices over the salmon, dot with 1½ tablespoons of the butter, and sprinkle with pepper. Cover the pan tightly with aluminum foil and bake for 20 minutes, or until the fish is cooked through at the thickest part. (If your fillets happen to be very thick, they may require up to 10 minutes longer cooking time.) Remove from the oven and transfer the fillets to a warm platter. Cut up the remaining 7½ tablespoons of butter and put it in a small saucepan. Add the cooking juices from the salmon and the mint. Stir over very low heat just until the butter is smooth and creamy. Serve the sauce in a sauceboat or spoon some over each portion of salmon.

6 SERVINGS

Cooking Fish

Fish steaks, such as salmon and swordfish, are best when broiled quickly—close to the heat—and moistened with butter and/or a marinade. Care should be taken not to overcook them or they will dry out. Fillet cuts, on the other hand, do best when cooked in the oven, usually at 375°, with a little butter and wine or lemon juice, in a pan that is tightly covered with foil. Average size salmon fillets will be done in 20 minutes (thin fillets, such as sole, will cook faster), and they will be very moist.

Suggested Menu

✂

*TORTELLINI IN BRODO

*SAUTÉED SOFT-SHELL CRABS

*SAUTÉED CHERRY TOMATOES
WITH BASIL

BOSTON LETTUCE AND
WATERCRESS SALAD

*FLUFFY LIME MOUSSE

SAUTÉED SOFT-SHELL CRABS

It only takes a few minutes to prepare this entrée, but it is a great delicacy, and looks particularly appetizing with a colorful side dish of sautéed cherry tomatoes and fresh basil. Soft-shell crabs are blue crabs that have shed their shells and have not yet grown new ones. After cleaning, the entire creature is edible. Native to the east coast of the United States, their season begins in May and extends through the summer months. They should be alive when purchased and can then be killed and cleaned by the fishmonger.

8 soft-shell crabs
Flour
5 tablespoons unsalted butter
2 tablespoons vegetable oil
¼ cup pine nuts
Fresh-ground pepper
2 tablespoons lemon juice

FOR THE GARNISH:

Parsley sprigs or watercress

Have the fishmonger kill and clean the crabs. Rinse them and pat dry. Dredge in flour. Heat 2 tablespoons of the butter and the oil in a very large skillet. Sauté the crabs for 3 minutes on each side over fairly high heat so that they brown nicely. Add the pine nuts to the pan during the last 2 minutes of cooking and shake the pan so that they color evenly. Transfer the crabs to warm plates, sprinkle with pepper, and scatter the nuts on top. Remove the pan from the heat and add the lemon juice and the remaining 3 tablespoons butter. Stir, off the heat, until the mixture is smooth and creamy in color and texture. Spoon over the crabs. Garnish each plate with parsley or watercress and, if desired, serve Sautéed Cherry Tomatoes with Basil (page 165) on the side.

4 SERVINGS

SHAD FILLETS

4-94. This works well, but needs more flavoring

Shad, available along the East Coast for just a few months in early spring, is a delicious fish—the equal, in my estimation, of salmon and brook trout. I have tried cooking it by several different methods and find that it is plumper, moister, and less oily when covered tightly and steamed in the oven. Allow ½ pound per serving. Cook the fillets according to the method described on page 101 for salmon fillets, moistening the fish with a little white wine rather than orange and lemon juice. Dot with butter and scatter a few minced shallots over and under the fish before cooking. Serve with the pan juices and lemon wedges.

SOLE AND SCALLOP RAGOUT

Serve with garlic bread and a green salad.

1 cup sliced yellow onions
1 large garlic clove, peeled
  and minced
6 small new potatoes, peeled
  and sliced ¼ inch thick
2 tablespoons olive oil
One 28-ounce can whole
  tomatoes, drained
½ cup minced fresh parsley
½ teaspoon dried basil

⅛ teaspoon dried
  thyme
Fresh-ground pepper
2 tablespoons well-
  drained capers
½ cup small pitted
  black olives
¼ cup tomato paste
1½ pounds sole fillets
¾ pound sea scallops
⅓ cup dry white wine

FOR THE GARNISH:

Minced fresh basil or parsley
Fresh-grated Parmesan cheese

In a large skillet, sauté the onions, garlic, and potatoes in the olive oil over low heat until the vegetables are tender but not brown, about 30 minutes. Add the tomatoes, breaking them up with a metal spoon. Stir in the parsley, basil, thyme, and pepper. Turn up the heat and cook, stirring occasionally, for several minutes until most of the moisture has evaporated. Do not let the tomatoes break down. Stir in the capers, olives, and tomato paste. (The recipe may be made ahead to this point.)

To complete the cooking, place the fish fillets on the bottom of the skillet. Put the scallops and vegetable mixture on top and pour in the wine. Cover the pan tightly and bring to a simmer. Cook, simmering very gently, for 5 to 8 minutes, or just until the fish and scallops are cooked through. Using a spatula, transfer the fish fillets, in large pieces, to large, warm soup plates. Spoon the scallops, vegetables, and broth on top. Sprinkle each serving with minced basil or parsley. Pass the Parmesan separately.

4 TO 6 SERVINGS

*If you have not used an entire can of to-
mato paste, store the remainder in a jar
or plastic container in the freezer. The
paste can be spooned out when needed
with little or no defrosting.*

Suggested Menu

PROSCIUTTO AND MELON

*STEAMED MUSSELS

*ITALIAN BREAD WITH ROAST PEPPERS,
MUSHROOMS, AND OLIVES

*WARM PEAR-AMARETTO PIE

STEAMED MUSSELS

A dish of mussels, quickly steamed open and served in their own wine-flavored broth, is as simple as it is delicious. Here, it is accompanied by a lemony sauce served separately, to be spooned in small quantities into each bowl of broth.

FOR THE SOUP:

5 pounds mussels
2 cups dry white wine
1 bay leaf
2 large garlic cloves, peeled and minced
¼ cup minced shallot or onion

FOR THE SAUCE:

4 tablespoons (½ stick) unsalted butter
1 medium garlic clove, peeled and minced
3½ tablespoons lemon juice
2 egg yolks

Scrub the mussels with a wire brush and pull off the beards. (If they don't come off easily, use a pair of pliers.) Put the wine, bay leaf, garlic, and shallot into a very large pot. Add the mussels, cover tightly, and bring the liquid to a boil. Cook for 5 to 8 minutes (depending on their size), or just until the mussels open wide. If there is no sediment or grit in the broth, it can be served directly from the cooking pot. If you are unsure about this, transfer the mussels with a slotted spoon to four large soup plates. Strain the broth into a bowl through a sieve lined with a paper towel, and then ladle the broth into the bowls.

While the mussels are cooking, make the sauce: Melt the butter in a small, heavy saucepan, add the garlic, and cook briefly to soften without browning. Mix the lemon juice and egg yolks and add to the pan, whisking over very low heat for 1 or 2 minutes until thickened. Turn the sauce into a small mustard pot or a bowl and let each person stir a spoonful into his or her broth, if desired.

4 SERVINGS

SWORDFISH IN AN ITALIAN MARINADE

For this recipe the swordfish is both marinated and broiled in a garlicky olive oil and lemon mixture. Prepared in this way, the swordfish steaks are amazingly moist and tender. There is virtually no work time involved, but you should allow a few hours for marinating.

> *One 2-pound swordfish steak (about 1 inch thick)*
> *¼ cup olive oil*
> *¼ cup lemon juice*
> *3 large garlic cloves, peeled and pressed*
> *¼ teaspoon dried basil*
> *⅛ teaspoon dried rosemary*
> *Fresh-ground pepper*
> *Approximately ⅓ cup chopped fresh basil leaves**

* If fresh basil is not available, substitute minced fresh parsley or mint.

Put the swordfish in a nonmetallic baking dish. (I use a 7-by-12-inch Pyrex dish.) Combine the oil, lemon juice, garlic, and dried herbs and pour over the steak. Sprinkle generously with pepper. Cover the pan with wax paper and refrigerate for several hours, turning over once during the marinating time.

Before cooking, allow the swordfish to return to room temperature. Preheat the broiler. Leave the fish in its marinade and broil very close to the heat, for about 4 minutes on each side for an inch-thick steak. Remove from the broiler as soon as it is cooked through. Scatter the chopped basil over the top of the fish and spoon the pan juices over each serving.

4 SERVINGS

Suggested Menu

*CREAM OF ARTICHOKE SOUP

*SWORDFISH WITH LIME, MINT,
AND TARRAGON SAUCE

*RICE SALAD WITH TOMATOES AND
FRESH HERBS

WATERCRESS

*QUICK BLACK CHERRY ICE CREAM

SWORDFISH WITH LIME, MINT, AND
TARRAGON SAUCE

The swordfish is broiled quickly and served with a delicately flavored butter sauce.

3½ to 4 pounds swordfish, cut into steaks 1 inch thick
1½ tablespoons unsalted butter
Lemon juice
Salt
Fresh-ground pepper

FOR THE SAUCE:

3 tablespoons lime juice
Grated zest of 1 lime
¼ cup minced fresh mint leaves
1 tablespoon chopped fresh tarragon or ¼ teaspoon dried
10 tablespoons (1 stick plus 2 tablespoons) unsalted butter

FOR THE GARNISH:

1 large bunch of watercress

Preheat the broiler. Put the swordfish in a buttered baking pan, dot with the 1½ tablespoons butter, and sprinkle with a little lemon juice, salt, and pepper. Broil close to the heating element for 5 minutes. Turn the fish over and broil for 2 to 3 minutes on the other side, or just until the fish is cooked through. Do not overcook or the fish will dry out.

While the swordfish is cooking, prepare the sauce: Put the lime juice, zest, mint, and tarragon in a small saucepan. Cut the butter into small pieces and add to the sauce. Keep the heat as low as possible and stir continuously until the butter is just melted. It should remain creamy in color and texture. Put the swordfish on individual plates, garnish with watercress, and spoon some of the sauce over each steak. If you are serving the swordfish from a platter, put the sauce in a sauceboat and serve it at the table.

8 SERVINGS

CHEESE SOUFFLÉ

A cheese soufflé is simplicity itself and, contrary to popular opinion, it is not difficult to make, although it is a last-minute operation. It is a good luncheon dish when you have guests. Serve it with a green salad and have berries or other fresh fruit for dessert. The recipe below is made with Jarlsberg cheese, but, if you like, you may substitute 6 to 8 ounces of sharp Cheddar cheese.

> *3 tablespoons unsalted butter*
> *¼ cup flour*
> *1½ cups milk*
> *6 egg yolks*
> *1½ cups grated Jarlsberg cheese (6 ounces)*
> *7 egg whites*
> *A pinch of cream of tartar*
> *3 to 4 tablespoons fresh-grated Parmesan cheese*

Preheat the oven to 400°. Generously butter an 8-cup soufflé dish.

Melt the butter in a heavy, 2-quart saucepan. Whisk in the flour, then gradually add the milk, whisking to blend. Turn up the heat and, stirring continuously, cook for a few minutes until the mixture comes to a boil and thickens. Remove from the heat and stir in the egg yolks, one at a time. Mix in the grated Jarlsberg. (The recipe may be made ahead to this point. If the cheese mixture has cooled off, rewarm, stirring over very low heat before proceeding, and preheat the oven to 400°.)

Beat the egg whites until frothy. Add the cream of tartar and continue beating only until the whites hold soft peaks. If they are too stiff, it will be difficult to fold them into the cheese mixture. Stir about one-quarter of the whites into the cheese base, then carefully fold in the rest. Turn into the soufflé dish and sprinkle the top with grated Parmesan. Place on the middle rack of the oven and turn the temperature down to 375°. Bake for 30 to 35 minutes. When done, the soufflé will have risen well above the rim of the dish and shrunk a bit from the sides. A knife inserted through the side of the soufflé and down into the center should test clean. Serve immediately.

4 TO 6 SERVINGS

Suggested Menu

*RED PEPPER AND ONION OMELET

*BAGUETTES WITH MELTED BRIE OR
BOILED NEW POTATOES

GREEN SALAD WITH FRESH BASIL

FRESH FRUIT

RED PEPPER AND ONION OMELET

This is a flat omelet, not the sort you flip over, and it is a hearty dish, composed of a quantity of sautéed onions and peppers lightly bound by eggs. Serve it with a green salad flavored with fresh basil, if it is available.

> *1 pound yellow onions, peeled and sliced thin (3 cups)*
> *2 medium-size sweet red peppers, seeded and sliced*
> *2 to 3 tablespoons vegetable oil*
> *4 eggs*
> *Salt*
> *Fresh-ground pepper*

Put the onions and peppers into a large, heavy skillet with the vegetable oil and sauté over moderate heat until the onions are soft and yellow. Do not brown. Briefly beat the eggs with a wire whisk and pour them over the vegetables. Cook just until set around the bottom and edges but still moist and slightly creamy in the center. Season with salt and pepper and serve immediately.

2 SERVINGS

EASY SAUCES FOR PASTA

Here are some ways to prepare pasta quickly, often with ingredients likely to be in your cupboard. When you have unexpected guests, or when there is no time or energy left for grocery shopping, a pasta dinner can be a great convenience.

To cook the pasta, bring a very large pot of water to a rolling boil. Then add a little vegetable oil (to keep the pasta from sticking together) and salt; put in the pasta and cook until tender but not too soft. Drain well in a colander, turn into a bowl, and toss with one of the following sauces. Spaghetti, fettuccine, fusilli, rigatoni, or almost any other shape can be used. Eight ounces of pasta will serve 3 or more, depending on the other ingredients in the recipe.

Quick Tomato Sauce   For 8 ounces pasta: Drain a 28-ounce can of tomatoes, reserving the juice, or use about 1¼ pounds peeled, fresh tomatoes. Put the tomatoes in a large skillet with 2 or 3 pressed garlic cloves, about ⅓ cup minced fresh parsley, and a little olive oil, and cook gently for 5 or 10 minutes, breaking up the tomatoes with a metal spoon. Toss with the cooked pasta, moistening with additional olive oil and a little of the reserved juice if you used canned tomatoes.

Clam or Tuna Sauce   For 8 ounces pasta: Heat in a saucepan ½ cup clam juice or chicken broth, ⅓ cup dry white wine, ¼ cup olive oil, 1 or 2 pressed garlic cloves, and some crumbled dried rosemary. Toss with the cooked pasta, then add 6 to 12 ounces minced canned clams or tuna, drained, and about ½ cup minced fresh parsley.

With Black Olives and Cream   For 8 to 12 ounces pasta: Moisten the cooked pasta with light cream and a little butter. Add a can of pitted black olives, well drained; fresh-ground pepper; and, if desired, some grated Parmesan.

With Artichokes   For 8 ounces pasta: Cook a package of frozen artichoke hearts, cut them in half, and add to the cooked pasta with enough light cream to moisten thoroughly, some grated Parmesan, minced fresh parsley, and, if desired, strips of ham.

With Parsley and Lemon   Toss the cooked pasta with enough olive oil and chicken broth to moisten well. Add grated lemon zest and plenty of minced fresh parsley.

Cream Sauce   Mix the cooked pasta with light cream, unsalted butter, and grated Parmesan. This is particularly good with fettuccine, linguine, or green noodles.

Chèvre Sauce   Combine the cooked pasta with light cream, unsalted butter, crumbled mild chèvre cheese (such as Montrachet), and fresh-ground pepper. Good with green noodles.

Carbonara   For 8 ounces thin spaghetti or fettuccine: Beat an egg yolk with ¼ cup light cream. Toss with the hot pasta and add enough additional cream to moisten well, 1 or 2 tablespoons unsalted butter, about 4 strips fried and crumbled bacon, some grated Parmesan, and fresh-ground pepper.

With Vegetables   Toss cooked thin spaghetti or fusilli with cooked peas, broccoli flowerets, cut-up asparagus, light cream, and unsalted butter. Serve grated Parmesan on the side.

Pesto Sauce   For 8 ounces thin spaghetti or fusilli: Mince 1 garlic clove, 1 cup packed fresh basil leaves, and ⅓ cup pine nuts in a food processor. Add ⅔ cup grated Parmesan and 1 tablespoon unsalted butter. With the motor running, add ½ cup olive oil in a thin stream. Mix with the cooked pasta. Moisten with extra olive oil if necessary. This is a rich and aromatic mixture. A milder and year-round version can be made by substituting fresh parsley sprigs for the basil.

With Mushrooms   Cook sliced, firm, white mushrooms in unsalted butter and add to cooked fettuccine with light cream, grated Parmesan, and, if desired, either black olives or strips of ham or crumbled bacon.

With Tomatoes and Mozzarella   Mix hot fusilli with peeled and chopped fresh tomatoes, diced mozzarella cheese, and olive oil. Allow to cool slightly and add chopped fresh basil leaves or minced parsley.

Spinach Sauce   For 8 ounces vermicelli or thin spaghetti: Partially defrost a 10-ounce package of chopped spinach and cook in 1 tablespoon butter in a large nonmetallic skillet or wide saucepan, stirring until the moisture evaporates. Or use fresh spinach and chop after it is cooked. Stir in 1 cup light cream, ½ cup sour cream, and, if desired, ¼ teaspoon dried basil and simmer for a few minutes. Toss with the cooked pasta.

Puttanesca Sauce   For 8 ounces thin spaghetti: In a large skillet, dissolve 3 anchovy fillets with 2 tablespoons minced fresh parsley and 3 to 4 minced garlic cloves in 2 tablespoons olive oil. Drain one 28-ounce can Italian tomatoes, reserving the juice. Add the tomatoes to the skillet and cook until most of their juice evaporates, cutting them into coarse pieces with a metal spoon. Add ⅔ cup small pitted black olives, 1 tablespoon capers, and about ½ cup of the reserved tomato juice, and simmer a few minutes to thicken. Toss the sauce with the cooked spaghetti. Add salt, pepper, a little olive oil if needed, and 2 tablespoons minced fresh parsley.

With Crabmeat Pick over 6 to 8 ounces fresh or frozen and defrosted crabmeat to remove any bits of shell. Cook 8 ounces thin spaghetti or thin noodles and toss with about ⅔ cup light cream, a little butter, 2 to 3 tablespoons lemon juice, 2 tablespoons minced fresh parsley, and the crabmeat.

Pasta Salads Cook 8 ounces fusilli, drain well, and while it is still warm, mix it with ½ cup olive oil and 3 tablespoons lemon juice. Let cool to room temperature and add chopped fresh tomatoes; plenty of chopped fresh basil, mint, or parsley; a little grated lemon zest; and whatever else appeals to you, such as black olives, feta cheese, strips of sweet red pepper, sliced avocado, etc.

To prevent a pot of water from boiling over, do not add salt until the water is boiling and you are ready to put in the food that you are cooking.

Cold Entrées

I have always considered summer the best season for entertaining. One can produce an elegant meal, drawing upon a rich variety of fresh fruits, vegetables, and herbs, without doing a bit of cooking after the guests arrive. The secret, of course, is to serve cold meals. Cold food can be imaginative and appetizing, and I have explored this topic more fully in an earlier book, *Cold Cuisine*. The recipes that follow have been developed since that book was published and add to the repertoire a number of entrée salads, as well as a cold beef fillet served with a mustard-caper sauce, marinated salmon fillets, and a cold roast chicken flavored with lime and tarragon.

Suggested Menu

*CHICKEN SALAD WITH CREAMY
HERB DRESSING

SLICED AVOCADOS VINAIGRETTE

WHOLE WHEAT TOAST TRIANGLES OR
*MINIATURE LIME MUFFINS

SEEDLESS GREEN GRAPES

*CREAMY CHOCOLATE BROWNIES

ENTRÉE SALADS

CHICKEN SALAD WITH CREAMY HERB DRESSING

The dressing for this salad is a lovely smooth combination of sour cream and mayonnaise, sparked with a little lemon juice and a great deal of fresh mint. Watercress adds a crisp flavor and texture to the salad.

FOR THE DRESSING:

¼ cup fresh parsley sprigs
¾ cup chopped fresh mint leaves
1 to 1½ tablespoons lemon juice
1 cup sour cream
¾ cup mayonnaise

FOR THE SALAD:

3 small whole chicken breasts, split in half (not boneless)
3 cups chicken broth
1 cup small pitted black olives
2 tablespoons chopped fresh chives or tender scallion ends
1 bunch of watercress, washed and trimmed

It is best to make the dressing several hours, or even a day ahead, to allow time for the mint flavor to develop. Mince the parsley and mint in a food processor. Add the lemon juice, sour cream, and mayonnaise and blend. (If you make the dressing by hand, beat it vigorously with a wire whisk or it will be too thick.) Turn into a bowl, cover, and refrigerate.

To poach the chicken breasts: Put them in a large skillet in a single layer with the broth. Partially cover and simmer gently for 17 minutes, or just until cooked through. Remove from the skillet and let cool on a platter. Remove the skin and bones and cut the chicken into strips about 3 inches long by ⅜ inch wide. Cover and refrigerate until serving.

Just before serving, put the chicken, olives, chives, and watercress in a salad bowl and toss with the dressing.

NOTE: If you mix the dressing with the salad ahead of time, the chicken will absorb too much of the dressing and the mixture will be too dry.)

6 SERVINGS

GENOA SALAD

FOR THE VINAIGRETTE:

> 6 *tablespoons olive oil*
> 2 *tablespoons lemon juice*
> 1 *tablespoon white wine vinegar*
> 1 *garlic clove, peeled and cut in half*

FOR THE SALAD:

6 ounces thin-sliced salami

One 2-ounce tin anchovy
fillets

½ pound mild feta cheese

½ pound mushrooms,
cleaned, trimmed, and
sliced

⅔ cup small pitted black
olives, cut in half

2 to 3 tablespoons
well-drained capers

¼ cup minced red onion

⅓ cup minced fresh
parsley

2 bunches of arugola*

1 pint cherry tomatoes

Fresh-ground pepper

* An Italian salad green, sold at special greengrocers. If it is not available, substitute watercress.

Combine the ingredients for the vinaigrette at least 1 hour before using to allow time for the garlic to marinate.

Cut the salami into ¼-inch-wide strips. Rinse the anchovies, pat dry with paper towels, and discard any visible bones. Crumble the feta cheese into coarse chunks, rinse in a colander under cold water, and drain on paper towels.

Combine the salami, anchovies, feta cheese, mushrooms, olives, capers, onions, and parsley in a salad bowl. Cover and refrigerate until 45 minutes before serving.

To serve: Wash the arugola carefully to remove all sand and trim off the root ends. Rinse the cherry tomatoes and cut them in half. Add the arugola and tomatoes to the salad and season with pepper. (Salt should not be necessary.) Discard the garlic clove and toss the vinaigrette with the salad. Serve at room temperature.

6 SERVINGS

Poaching Chicken Breasts
Care should be taken when poaching chicken breasts for use in a salad or casserole, as overcooked chicken will be dry and stringy. Simmer gently in the poaching liquid, do not boil, and turn over halfway through cooking. Chicken breast halves with the skin and bones will be done in 17 to 20 minutes, boneless breasts in half the time. Cut the flesh at the thickest part to check. As soon as it is no longer pink, take it out of the poaching broth and set on a platter to cool.

You can make a good soup stock by adding chicken bouillon cubes to the poaching water. Use 1 cube for every cup or cup and a half of water. After the chicken has been cooked, strain the poaching liquid into a jar, let cool to room temperature, label, and freeze until needed. Do not remove the layer of fat from the surface until you use the stock, as the fat helps to preserve it.

Suggested Menu

*MEDITERRANEAN SALAD

TOASTED MAROUK OR SAHARA BREAD

CHÈVRE CHEESE AND FRESH CHERRIES
OR GRAPES

MEDITERRANEAN SALAD

This is a hearty composed salad similar to a salade Niçoise. It is full of pungent flavors including roasted red peppers, basil, capers, and anchovies.

FOR THE VINAIGRETTE:

½ cup olive oil
2 tablespoons wine vinegar
1 small garlic clove, peeled and pressed
1 teaspoon Dijon or Düsseldorf mustard

FOR THE SALAD:

1½ pounds small red-
skinned new potatoes
½ cup thin-sliced red onion
½ pound green beans,
trimmed
2 large sweet red peppers
(1 pound)
One 2-ounce tin of
anchovy fillets

12 Calamata olives,
halved and pitted
2 tablespoons well-
drained capers
¾ cup chopped fresh
basil*
Fresh-ground pepper

* If fresh basil is not available, substitute about ⅓ cup minced fresh parsley.

Whisk together the ingredients for the vinaigrette.

Boil the potatoes until they are tender. While they are still warm, peel and slice them ¼ inch thick, then toss them with the vinaigrette in a large, shallow bowl. Mix in the sliced onion.

Cook the beans in about an inch of salted water in a saucepan with a tight-fitting lid until tender but not soft. (Check after 7 minutes.) Drain in a colander, refresh under cold running water, and turn onto paper towels to absorb excess moisture. Toss with the potato mixture.

Place the peppers on a baking sheet about 4 inches below a pre-heated broiler and cook until the skin blackens, turning to char all sides. Let cool slightly, then peel them under cold running water, discarding the stems and seeds. Cut into ½-inch strips and pat dry. Rinse the anchovies and dry on paper towels. Add the peppers, anchovies, olives, capers, and basil to the salad, and season to taste with pepper. Serve at room temperature.

4 SERVINGS

MUSSEL, RICE, AND ROAST PEPPER SALAD

I particularly like this version of mussel and rice salad. The roasted sweet red pepper adds a bright flavor as well as color to the combination.

FOR THE VINAIGRETTE:

½ cup olive oil
¼ cup lemon juice
1 small garlic clove, peeled

4 pounds mussels
3 garlic cloves, peeled and
    cut in half
2/3 cup dry white wine
2 large sweet red peppers
1 1/3 cups rice
1/4 cup minced fresh
    parsley

1/3 cup chopped fresh
    basil, if available
3 tablespoons minced
    scallions with tender
    green ends
Salt
Fresh-ground pepper

Combine the oil and lemon juice for the vinaigrette. Grate a little
of the garlic into the mixture, then drop in the rest of the clove.

Scrub the mussels well under running water and remove the
beards. Put them into a large, heavy pot with the garlic and wine.
Cover, bring to a boil, and cook for 5 minutes, or just until the
shells open wide. (Discard any that fail to open.) Remove the
mussels and shell them. Strain the mussel broth through a sieve lined
with a damp towel and reserve 1/4 cup plus 2 tablespoons.

Preheat the broiler. Put the peppers in a pan about 4 inches
below the heat source and broil until the skin blisters and blackens,
turning to char all sides. When cool enough to handle, peel off the
skin under cold running water, discarding the core and seeds. Pat
dry and cut into strips 1 to 1 1/2 inches wide.

Bring a very large pot of water to a rolling boil. Add a little salt
and the rice and cook for 17 minutes, or until the rice is tender but
firm. Drain well in a colander, rinse under hot tap water, and turn
into a salad bowl. Toss with the vinaigrette (discarding the garlic
clove) while the rice is still warm. Let cool to room temperature,
then mix in the mussels, peppers, the reserved mussel broth, the
parsley, basil, and scallions. Season with a little salt, if necessary,
and plenty of pepper. Serve either slightly chilled or at room
temperature.

6 SERVINGS

Suggested Menu

*SEASHELL SALAD

*OPEN-FACE CUCUMBER SANDWICHES

*MELON WITH GINGER

*VEE'S SHORTBREAD

SEASHELL SALAD

Scallops and shell pasta mixed with tomatoes and herbs in a mustardy vinaigrette.

FOR THE DRESSING:

> *6 tablespoons olive oil*
> *3 tablespoons lemon juice*
> *1 tablespoon Dijon mustard*

FOR THE SALAD:

> *Salt*
> *Vegetable oil*
> *4 ounces small pasta shells*
> *(¾-inch size)*
> *1½ cups cherry tomatoes,*
> *cut in half*
> *2½ tablespoons minced*
> *scallions with tender*
> *green ends*
> *½ cup chopped fresh*
> *mint leaves*
> *2 tablespoons minced*
> *fresh parsley*

> *Grated zest of 1 large*
> *lemon*
> *1 pound sea scallops*
> *1 tablespoon unsalted*
> *butter*
> *1 tablespoon lemon*
> *juice*
> *Fresh-ground pepper*
> *1 bunch of watercress*
> *or arugola, washed*
> *and trimmed*

Combine the ingredients for the dressing and reserve.

Bring a very large pot of water to a boil. Add salt, a little vegetable oil, and the pasta. Cook until tender but still firm. Drain well in a colander, turn into a bowl, and toss with the vinaigrette. Let cool to room temperature, then add the tomatoes, scallions, mint, parsley, and lemon zest.

Rinse the scallops and dry on paper towels. Cut in half if they are very large. Melt the butter in a large skillet. Add the scallops, sprinkle with the lemon juice, and cook over moderate heat, stirring occasionally, for 2 or 3 minutes, or just until cooked through. Do not overcook. Let cool to room temperature, then add the scallops and cooking juices to the salad. Cover and refrigerate until serving. Just before serving, toss with the watercress or arugola.

4 SERVINGS

Suggested Menu

JELLIED MADRILÈNE

*STEAK SALAD

*HERB AND PARMESAN BREAD

*PECAN PIE

STEAK SALAD

FOR THE VINAIGRETTE:

¾ cup olive oil
3 tablespoons red wine vinegar
1 small garlic clove, peeled and pressed or grated
1 tablespoon Dijon mustard

FOR THE SALAD:

3½ pounds sirloin steak with bone in or 3 pounds
  boneless (1½ inches thick)
15 slices bacon
3 medium-large tomatoes (1½ pounds), peeled,
  cored, and sliced
½ cup thin-sliced red onion
3 tablespoons well-drained capers
1½ cups chopped fresh basil
Salt
Fresh-ground pepper

Combine the ingredients for the vinaigrette and reserve.

Broil the steak for about 8 minutes on each side for rare meat. Let cool to room temperature and reserve.

Broil or fry the bacon until crisp, drain on paper towels, and crumble coarse. Slice the steak into thin strips and toss in a salad bowl with the vinaigrette to prevent the meat from darkening. Add the bacon, tomatoes, onion, capers, basil, and seasoning to the salad just before serving.

6 SERVINGS

TORTELLINI, TOMATO, AND BASIL SALAD

Good tortellini can be bought fresh in pasta stores, or frozen, or dried and packed in boxes (Amore and Ferrara are good brands). This salad is a colorful medley that includes cherry tomatoes, black olives, and basil, as well as the tortellini. It can be prepared ahead and served as a light entrée for a summer lunch or supper, or as an appetizer.

FOR THE VINAIGRETTE:

> *¾ cup olive oil*
> *3 tablespoons lemon juice*
> *1 garlic clove, peeled and cut in half*

FOR THE SALAD:

> *14 to 16 ounces cheese- or spinach-filled tortellini*
> *Salt*
> *Vegetable oil*
> *1½ to 2 cups chopped fresh basil*
> *1 pint cherry tomatoes*
> *4 ounces feta cheese (optional)*
> *One 6-ounce can small pitted black olives, well drained*
> *Fresh-ground pepper*

Combine the ingredients for the vinaigrette at least 1 hour before cooking the pasta.

Bring a very large pot of water to a rolling boil. Add the tortellini and a little salt and vegetable oil. Boil until tender but not too soft. Drain well in a colander and turn into a salad bowl. Discard the garlic clove and pour the vinaigrette over the warm pasta. Mix in about ½ cup of the basil. Let cool to room temperature.

Shortly before serving, rinse and stem the cherry tomatoes and cut them in half. If you are using feta cheese, break it up into chunks, place in a colander, and rinse under cold tap water. Drain well on paper towels and add to the salad with the cherry tomatoes, olives, the remaining basil, and the pepper. Serve at room temperature.

6 ENTRÉE OR 10 APPETIZER SERVINGS

Suggested Menu

*CHILLED CARROT AND PEACH SOUP

*COLD BEEF FILLET WITH
CAPER-MUSTARD SAUCE

SLICED TOMATOES WITH WATERCRESS

*STRAWBERRY CHARLOTTE

OTHER COLD ENTRÉES

COLD BEEF FILLET WITH CAPER-MUSTARD SAUCE

Because it is served cold, the beef can be cooked a day ahead, but do not slice it until shortly before serving or it will lose its pink color.

> *One 4-pound beef tenderloin*
> *Salt*
> *Fresh-ground pepper*
> *Ground allspice or ground ginger*

FOR THE SAUCE:

> *1 egg yolk*
> *1 scant tablespoon Dijon mustard*
> *½ cup fine, light olive oil*
> *2 teaspoons lemon juice*
> *2 tablespoons minced fresh parsley*
> *2 tablespoons chopped capers*

FOR THE GARNISH:

> *Watercress*

To cook the beef: Preheat the oven to 500°. Put the beef in a roasting pan and sprinkle with salt, pepper, and a little allspice or ginger. As soon as you put the meat in the oven, turn down the temperature to 225°. For rare meat, cook until a meat thermometer registers 145°. The cooking time will vary according to the thickness of the meat. A very thin tenderloin may take only 35 minutes, but the average size will require 1 to 1¼ hours cooking time. When the meat is done, let cool to room temperature, then cover with plastic wrap and refrigerate.

To make the sauce: Combine the egg yolk and mustard in a small bowl. While beating continuously with a wire whisk, add the olive oil, at first drop by drop and then in a very thin stream as the mixture thickens, to make a mayonnaise. After the oil is absorbed, stir in the lemon juice, parsley, and capers. Cover and refrigerate until serving.

To serve: Slice the meat ¼ inch thick and arrange it in an overlapping row in the middle of a platter. Spoon a thin strip of sauce down the center of the slices. Garnish the platter with a border of watercress and serve the rest of the sauce in a sauceboat.

8 TO 10 SERVINGS

Cooking Rare Beef
When a large roast of beef, such as a tenderloin, is to be served rare, it is best to cook it in a slow oven, usually 225°. This method produces an evenly cooked roast, each slice uniformly pink or rare from the center to the outside edge, rather than having a wide band of well-done meat surrounding a bloody center. The preceding recipe for Cold Beef Fillet with Caper-Mustard Sauce demonstrates this method.

Suggested Menu

DEVILED EGGS

*COLD ROAST CHICKEN WITH LIME
AND TARRAGON

*TOMATO ASPIC WITH
*SOUR-CREAM—CHIVE SAUCE

*BUTTERMILK BISCUITS

*DEEP-DISH PEACH PIE

COLD ROAST CHICKEN WITH LIME AND TARRAGON

This is an easy dish to prepare for guests, since the cooking is done ahead of time. The chicken meat is imbued with the flavors of lime and fresh tarragon, and so while it is a simple dish, it is not ordinary. It is best to roast the chickens whole so that they retain their juices. Do not refrigerate them after cooking (unless you have leftovers) as this spoils their flavor and texture. If they are intended for the evening meal, cook them in mid to late afternoon and hold at room temperature until serving.

> *Two 3-pound chickens*
> *½ cup lime juice*
> *5 tablespoons chopped fresh tarragon*
> *6 tablespoons (¾ stick) unsalted butter, softened*
> *Salt*
> *Fresh-ground pepper*

FOR THE GARNISH:

> *Fresh parsley sprigs*

Early in the day, rinse the chickens, removing any loose fat, and dry with paper towels. Put them in an enameled roasting pan and pour the lime juice over the birds and inside their cavities. Marinate all day in the refrigerator, turning them once or twice in the lime juice.

Late in the afternoon (3:00 to 5:00 depending on serving time), pour off the marinade and reserve. Preheat the oven to 375°. Pat the chickens dry and return to the roasting pan. Combine the chopped tarragon with 4 tablespoons of the softened butter. Put about a teaspoon of the mixture into the cavity of each chicken. Insert the rest underneath the skin, spreading it with a blunt knife or your fingers to cover as large an area as possible. Truss the birds and rub with the remaining 2 tablespoons butter. Sprinkle with salt and pepper and place each bird on its side. Roast for 30 minutes on one side and then 25 minutes on the other side, basting with the reserved lime juice and the pan juices after the birds start to brown. Turn breast side up and roast 5 to 10 minutes longer to complete browning. The birds are done when the thigh juices run clear. Remove from the oven and let cool to room temperature, basting occasionally with the pan juices as they cool. Let stand at room temperature until ready to serve.

To serve, carve the chickens or cut them into quarters, discarding the backbone. Place on a platter, garnished with sprigs of parsley. Skim the fat from the pan juices and serve the juices in a small pitcher, at room temperature or slightly warmed. The Sour-Cream–Chive Sauce (page 168) prepared for the Tomato Aspic is also good with the chicken.

6 TO 8 SERVINGS

MARINATED SALMON STEAKS WITH GREEN MAYONNAISE

Cold salmon is one of the delights of summer. For this recipe, the salmon is poached, marinated, and served with Green Mayonnaise on the side. It is a lovely dish to look at, as well as to eat.

4 salmon steaks, cut about 1 inch thick
2 cups water
⅔ cup dry white wine
A few sprigs of fresh parsley or dill

FOR THE MARINADE:

¼ cup olive oil
1½ tablespoons lemon juice
1 teaspoon white wine vinegar

FOR THE GARNISH:

Capers
Branches of fresh dill or parsley
4 lemon wedges

Green Mayonnaise (recipe follows)

Put the salmon, water, wine, and herbs in a heavy skillet, partially cover, and adjust the heat so that the liquid barely simmers. Poach for 12 to 15 minutes, or just until the steaks are cooked through, turning them over once halfway through cooking. Be careful not to overcook or the fish will be dry. Transfer with a slotted spatula to a shallow dish. Drain off any poaching liquid that accumulates in the dish. Combine the ingredients for the marinade and pour over the salmon while it is still warm. Allow to marinate for a few hours, at room temperature, turning once or twice.

Serve the salmon at room temperature. Remove it from the marinade and sprinkle a scant teaspoonful of capers over each serving. Garnish with sprigs of dill or parsley and the lemon wedges. Serve the Green Mayonnaise on the side.

4 SERVINGS

GREEN MAYONNAISE

3 tablespoons fresh mint
   leaves
1½ tablespoons fresh
   tarragon
1½ tablespoons fresh
   parsley sprigs
1½ tablespoons chopped
   fresh chives
2 egg yolks

1 tablespoon plus 2
   teaspoons lemon
   juice
1 tablespoon Dijon
   mustard
¾ cup light olive oil
¾ cup vegetable oil
Salt

Mince the herbs in a food processor or blender. Add the egg yolks, lemon juice, and mustard to the work bowl. Combine the olive oil and vegetable oil in a 2-cup Pyrex measure. With the motor running, add the oil, at first drop by drop and then, as the mayonnaise thickens, in a thin stream. Add salt to taste.

NOTE: This mayonnaise can be made by hand, using a wire whisk or electric mixer, as in the recipe for Dill Mayonnaise on page 12. The herbs must be minced very fine, and the mayonnaise will be speckled with green rather than uniformly tinted.

ABOUT 1½ CUPS

Individual egg whites can be stored in plastic ice cube trays and frozen. Cover with foil and an airtight plastic bag to prevent a freezer taste.

Suggested Menu

*STEAK TARTARE CASANOVA

*ARUGOLA, MUSHROOM, AND
ENDIVE SALAD

TOASTED FRENCH BREAD

FRESH RASPBERRIES

STEAK TARTARE CASANOVA

On a recent trip to Italy, we had a splendid lunch in the Casanova Grill at the Palace Hotel in Milan—steak tartare, arugola salad, fresh raspberries, and a delicious Antinori wine. The waiter prepared the steak tartare at the table, and it was the best version of that dish I've had. A close reproduction of his recipe follows.

2 egg yolks
1 tablespoon Düsseldorf or Dijon mustard
1 tablespoon lemon juice
1 teaspoon Worcestershire sauce
⅓ cup olive oil
1½ pounds fresh-ground lean top round, flank, or sirloin steak

1½ tablespoons fine-minced fresh parsley
1½ tablespoons chopped capers
1½ tablespoons fine-minced onion
2 small anchovy fillets, minced fine
Salt
Fresh-ground pepper

FOR THE GARNISH:

Fresh parsley sprigs
Lemon wedges

In a small bowl, whisk together the egg yolks, mustard, lemon juice, and Worcestershire sauce. Add the olive oil, whisking to blend. (Do not make a mayonnaise; just combine the ingredients.)

Put the ground beef into a large bowl, pour the sauce over it, add the remaining ingredients, and combine well. (This is most easily done with a large 2-pronged fork from a carving set.) Cover tightly with plastic wrap and refrigerate until serving.

Garnish each portion with parsley sprigs and a lemon wedge and serve toasted, thin-sliced French bread on the side.

4 SERVINGS

Vegetables, Side Dishes, & Salads

In writing this chapter, I was more concerned with the proper method of cooking various vegetables than with new and fancy recipes for them. Most fresh green vegetables are best served simply. Care should be taken to cook them for the proper length of time so that they retain maximum flavor and just the right amount of texture. They often need little more embellishment than butter and lemon juice. I have found that vegetables such as green beans, Brussels sprouts, broccoli, and asparagus will retain their bright green color if cooked airtight (without lifting the lid too often to check on their progress) in a little salted water or in a steamer basket.

The chapter includes some unfamiliar and very easy ways of preparing other vegetables, such as a quick skillet method of cooking cabbage that renders it sweet, nutty, and unlike the common view of this vegetable (which deserves more respect than it usually gets). From Elizabeth David's cookbooks (which I read and reread with increasing enjoyment), I have learned that both onions and beets can be baked whole in the oven. Treated in this way, they taste far better than when subjected to elaborate preparations; and the method, of course, could not be simpler.

The salads that conclude this chapter fall into two categories: starchy salads, such as potato, rice, or white bean salad, all of which should be served with the main course; and light, refreshing salads composed of greens, tomatoes, or, in one case, avocado and cantaloupe, which should accompany or follow the entrée but not precede it, unless it is the sort of salad that could double as an appetizer.

VEGETABLES AND
SIDE DISHES

BABY CARROTS BRAISED WITH ORANGE AND GINGER

2 pounds baby carrots
2½ tablespoons unsalted butter
1¼ teaspoons grated peeled fresh gingerroot
½ cup orange juice
½ cup chicken broth

Scrape the carrots and cut off the stem ends. Melt the butter in a large skillet and add the carrots and gingerroot. Cook over low heat for a few minutes, stirring. Add the orange juice and chicken broth, cover the pan tightly, and simmer gently for 20 minutes, or until the carrots are tender but firm. Do not let them get soft. Remove the lid from the pan. If much liquid remains, turn up the heat and boil quickly to reduce to 2 or 3 tablespoons.

NOTE: If preparing ahead, reheat in a 350° oven for about 15 minutes in a covered baking dish.

6 TO 8 SERVINGS

BAKED BEETS

This is an uncommon way of serving beets, but it is an easy and delicious one. The beets retain more flavor when baked than when they are boiled.

Choose large, fresh beets, about 2½ inches in diameter, and allow 1 per serving. Scrub them carefully under running water with a vegetable brush, but do not peel. Cut off the stem ends and any trailing roots. Place them in a shallow pan and bake at 350° for 2½ to 3 hours, or until a skewer pierces the beets very easily. They should be quite tender. Unless you have time to spare, serve them unpeeled, letting each person peel his or her own at the table.

BROCCOLI

When buying broccoli, allow ½ pound per person.

Wash well and peel the heavy stems with a vegetable parer. Trim off the stem ends (or cut off most of the stems and reserve for making soup) and separate the heads into manageable sections. Place in a pot with a tight-fitting lid and add about an inch of water and a little salt. Cover tightly and bring to a boil. Lower the heat so that the liquid simmers and cook for 5 to 10 minutes, or until tender. Drain well and toss in a warm serving bowl with a little melted butter and lemon juice.

BUTTERED CABBAGE

Cabbage cooked in this manner, rather than boiled, has a surprisingly sweet and nutty flavor.

1 medium cabbage
3 tablespoons unsalted butter
Salt
Fresh-ground pepper

Cut the cabbage into quarters and cut out the core. Slice each quarter lengthwise, then crosswise into ¾-inch pieces. Place in a colander and rinse well under cold running water. Put the cabbage, with the water clinging to the leaves, in a very large skillet with a tight-fitting lid. Cover and steam over low heat for 15 to 25 minutes, or just until tender. The thicker leaves should be a bit crisp. (The recipe may be prepared ahead to this point.)

If you are not serving the cabbage right away, uncover and let cool to room temperature. To serve, add the butter to the pan and reheat the cabbage over moderate heat, stirring often. Do not overcook. Sprinkle with a little salt and pepper and serve immediately.

6 TO 8 SERVINGS

CORN ON THE COB

Corn should be eaten as soon as possible after it is picked, so it is best purchased at a farm market, where it is grown on the premises and picked several times a day. You will discover your own favorite varieties; those I like best (available in the Northeast) are Sweet Sal, Spring Gold, Silver Queen, and Burgundy Delight.

Shuck the corn just before cooking. Bring a very large pot of water to a rolling boil, then add salt and, if you like, a little sugar. Put in the corn and boil hard for 3 to 5 minutes, if it is very fresh. (Older corn will take a bit longer.) Test for tenderness by poking a metal skewer into a kernel. Transfer with tongs to a bowl and serve with unsalted butter.

CREAMED SPINACH

This is a simplified version of creamed spinach that does not require making a separate cream sauce.

Four 10-ounce packages spinach, fresh or frozen,
*   chopped*
2 tablespoons unsalted butter, softened
2 tablespoons flour
1 cup heavy cream, or ½ cup sour cream and
*   ½ cup heavy cream*
Salt
Fresh-ground pepper

If you are using fresh spinach, wash it well in a sinkful of water, discarding the stems and any wilted leaves. Pack the spinach into a large pot with just the water clinging to the leaves. Cover tightly and cook until wilted, turning and stirring once or twice. Drain well in a colander, pressing out as much moisture as possible. Chop it coarse and transfer to an enameled or stainless-steel skillet. (If using frozen spinach, defrost it in the package and drain off the water. Put it into an enameled or stainless-steel skillet, and cook over high heat for a few minutes to evaporate the moisture.)

Blend the softened butter with the flour and stir into the spinach. Add the cream or sour cream and cream, and seasoning to taste, and cook, stirring, for a minute or two until thickened.

NOTE: This recipe may be made ahead and reheated in a covered casserole at 350° for about 15 minutes.

6 TO 8 SERVINGS

CRUSTY POTATOES

This is a variation on the classic Potatoes Anna—baked with butter in a hot oven so that the bottom is crisp and browned. In this version, I've flavored the potatoes with Parmesan cheese. This dish goes particularly well with roast beef or lamb.

3 pounds Idaho potatoes
Fresh-ground pepper
4 tablespoons (½ stick) unsalted butter, melted
⅔ cup grated Parmesan cheese

Generously butter a 9-by-13- or 10-by-14-inch baking pan. Peel the potatoes and slice thin, ⅛ inch or thinner, and as they are sliced, drop them into a bowl of cold water. Drain the potatoes and dry well on paper towels. Place a single layer of potato slices in the pan and sprinkle with pepper, some of the melted butter, and some of the cheese. Continue layering in this way, ending with a layer of cheese. (The dish may be prepared several hours ahead to this point.)

Preheat the oven to 425° and adjust the oven shelf to the lowest level. Bake the potatoes, uncovered, for 35 to 40 minutes, or until crusty on the bottom and golden brown on top. If the potatoes are tender, but the top is not browned, place under the broiler for a minute.

NOTE: This recipe can be finished up to 2 hours ahead of serving. Keep the potatoes warm by loosely covering the pan with aluminum foil and reheat for 5 to 10 minutes before serving in an oven preheated to 425°. This method is useful if you are cooking a roast at a lower temperature and have only one oven.

6 SERVINGS

On Baking Potatoes
A potato will bake faster if you insert a metal skewer through it. Scrub the potato well and place on the oven rack without any covering so that the skin will be crisp. Russet potatoes (not to be confused with red-skinned) look much like Idaho potatoes, but have a much better, somewhat sweeter, flavor. They are excellent for baking and are in season during the late spring and summer months.

GREEN BEANS

Do not be tempted to buy green beans if they are not absolutely fresh. They should look smooth and crisp (test by snapping one in half) and be small in size. Large ones tend to be tough. The season for green beans is spring and early summer; be cautious of them as the summer advances. Cooked tightly covered, they will retain their fresh, bright color. Use a heavy lid so that your pot will be airtight.

> 1 ½ *pounds fresh green beans*
> *Salt*
> 1 ½ *tablespoons unsalted butter*

Rinse the beans and snap off the stem ends. Put them in a very heavy saucepan (enameled iron is best) with about an inch of water and a little salt. Cover tightly with a heavy lid and cook at a low boil for 7 to 15 minutes, or just until the beans are tender but still a bit crisp. Drain them well, turn into a serving dish, and toss with the butter.

6 SERVINGS

GREEN NOODLES WITH PARMESAN

This is a good side dish for many chicken and fish entrées.

> *Salt*
> *Vegetable oil*
> *8 ounces thin green noodles*

> *3 tablespoons unsalted butter*
> *⅓ cup light cream*
> *½ cup fresh-grated Parmesan cheese*
> *Fresh-ground pepper*

Bring a very large pot of water to a rolling boil. Add a little salt and vegetable oil and the noodles, and boil until tender but still firm. Drain well in a colander and toss with the remaining ingredients.

4 SERVINGS

PEAS

To cook fresh peas: Boil them in salted water to cover for 5 to 20 minutes, depending on their size and maturity. (Early spring peas are the most tender, and they get progressively tougher as the season advances.) Drain well, toss with butter, and serve.

I discovered this method for cooking frozen peas when preparing a dish of pasta mixed with vegetables. I had partially defrosted a package of Bird's Eye "tiny, tender peas" and I decided to simplify matters by putting them in a long-handled strainer and dipping this into the boiling pasta water. I submerged them for only a few seconds, and they were done. This is an effortless way of cooking peas, and they turn out particularly plump and fresh tasting.

To cook: Bring a large pot of water to a rolling boil. Add salt and dip in the peas as described above. Partially defrosted peas will be done in 5 to 10 seconds. Transfer to a warm serving dish and toss with a lump of butter and a squirt of lemon juice, if desired. (See page 161 for a skillet method of cooking frozen peas.)

SUGAR SNAP PEAS

These peas have a tender, edible pod, like snow peas or Chinese pea pods, but are much sweeter and plumper. To prepare them when fresh, pull off the stem and, with it, the string that runs along the inside curve of the pod. Rinse and place in a steamer basket. Cover the pan tightly and cook over boiling water until the pods are tender, but still a bit crisp. The cooking time for fresh sugar snap peas is 7 to 10 minutes.

Frozen sugar snap peas can be cooked in the same way, but should be steamed for only a minute or two. (They will not need stemming or stringing.) Or they can be partially defrosted and cooked in a large skillet, as in the following recipe.

TINY PEAS AND SUGAR SNAP PEAS

The "tiny, tender" frozen peas packaged by Bird's Eye are surprisingly sweet and fresh tasting. Prepare them by defrosting for an hour or two at room temperature before cooking. To cook, use a fairly large skillet to allow the moisture to evaporate. Stir over moderate heat for a few minutes until heated through. Don't overcook or they will shrivel. If any moisture remains, drain in a strainer and return to the pan. Add a lump of butter and, if desired, a squirt of lemon juice.

Frozen sugar snap peas can be cooked in the same way. Try mixing them with tiny, tender peas. They take about the same length of time to cook. An 8-ounce package of each will serve 6 generously.

NEW POTATOES AND SUGAR SNAP PEAS

This is a fine summer vegetable dish, which we were served at the home of our friends, Joe and U. T. Summers, and which I've since made in my own kitchen. Here is the recipe as U. T. passed it on to me:

> The vegetable recipe is Aunt Alice Filkins's adaptation of the old family requirement of fresh peas and new potatoes from the garden for the Fourth of July in Beaver, Pennsylvania. She steams about 2½ pounds of new potatoes, cut to about the size of the potatoes she remembers, leaving the skin on; adds a large quartered onion; and tests them for doneness in 20 minutes. During the last 4 minutes of cooking, add 1 pound of washed and strung pop [sugar snap] peas. Add butter, salt, and pepper to taste.
>
> Aunt Alice, by the way, is ninety-two and lives alone in her own apartment in Houston now. She has learned to use her steamer and prefers it to her mother's method of boiling.

SERVES 6

How to Cook Rice

My best advice for cooking rice is not to follow the package directions, unless you like it gummy. I have found two methods to be successful, producing rice that has firm and separate grains.

1. Boiling: Use this method for dry, fluffy rice. Fill a very large pot (at least 8-quart capacity) with water. Cover and bring to a rolling boil. After the water boils, remove the lid and add a little salt and the rice and boil until tender but still firm. Long-grain rice will be done in 17 minutes. Drain in a colander, and rinse with very hot tap water.

2. Braising: Use this method for buttery, moist rice. Put the raw rice into a fine sieve or colander and rinse well with cold tap water to remove excess starch. Melt a little butter in a heavy saucepan (enameled iron is best) and cook the rice gently for a few minutes in the butter. For every cup of rice, add 2 cups of water or chicken stock or canned chicken broth (not bouillon cubes) to the pan. Cover tightly and bring to a simmer. Simmer gently for 17 to 20 minutes. When cooked, the rice should be tender but not soft, and most of the liquid should be absorbed. If too much liquid remains in the pan, boil for a minute to evaporate. Stir in a little extra butter, if desired.

ORANGE RICE

This is a good accompaniment to Veal Shanks Braised with Artichokes (page 92) or any roast meat or fowl. You can make Lemon Rice by substituting the zest of 1 large or 2 small lemons for the orange zest.

> *2 cups long-grain rice*
> *4 tablespoons (½ stick) unsalted butter*
> *4 cups chicken stock or canned broth*
> *Grated zest of 2 large navel or Valencia oranges*
> *2 tablespoons minced fresh parsley (optional)*

Put the rice in a fine strainer and rinse well under cold running water.

Melt 2 tablespoons of the butter in a heavy saucepan (preferably enameled iron). Add the rice and cook, stirring, for 1 or 2 minutes. Pour in the stock and bring to a simmer. Cover the pan tightly and simmer over low heat for 17 to 20 minutes, or just until the rice is tender. Remove the lid and cook, uncovered, for a minute or two if all the broth is not absorbed. Remove from the heat and stir in the remaining butter, the orange zest, and, if desired, the parsley.

10 SERVINGS

> *A good-quality lemon zester is an excellent tool for quickly and efficiently grating the zest from citrus fruit without cutting into the bitter white pith. It can also be used to make fine shreds for garnish.*

ROAST ONIONS

This method of cooking onions is described by Elizabeth David in *Mediterranean Cooking*, one of her many splendid books. Cooked in this manner, the onions are tender, sweet, and full of flavor. It is an amazingly easy recipe—no more trouble than baking a potato—and friends are always intrigued by the novelty of onions served in this manner.

Choose 1 large yellow onion (about 3 inches in diameter) for each serving. Wipe clean with a damp cloth or rinse quickly and dry. Preheat the oven to 350°. Place the unpeeled onions in a baking pan. Bake for 1½ hours, or until very tender. Remove from the pan and peel off the outer skin or let each guest peel his own. They can be seasoned with salt and pepper at the table, and they can be served with a lump of butter as well, but I prefer them plain, as they have their own moist, buttery quality.

SAUTÉED CHERRY TOMATOES WITH BASIL

A colorful side dish to brighten up a dinner plate.

1 pint cherry tomatoes
2 tablespoons unsalted butter
⅔ cup chopped fresh basil

Rinse, stem, and dry the tomatoes. Heat the butter in a skillet, add the tomatoes, and cook over moderate heat for 3 to 5 minutes, stirring frequently, until tender but not soft. Do not cook so long that the skins break. Remove from the heat, add the basil, and stir to blend.

4 SERVINGS

TOMATO ASPIC WITH SOUR-CREAM–CHIVE SAUCE

This is a lovely, cooling side dish to serve in summer with an entrée such as Cold Roast Chicken with Lime and Tarragon (page 144). The aspic has a bright, pure tomato taste and is served with a Sour-Cream–Chive Sauce on the side.

*Two 28-ounce cans
    tomatoes, packed in purée*
*2 garlic cloves, peeled and
    sliced*
1 bay leaf
3 whole cloves
Salt
Fresh-ground pepper
*1 tablespoon minced fresh
    dill or ⅛ teaspoon dried
    dill weed*

*1½ tablespoons
    minced fresh chives*
*2 envelopes plus 1½
    teaspoons unflavored
    gelatin*
*½ cup plus 1
    tablespoon cold
    water*
*1½ tablespoons lemon
    juice*

FOR THE GARNISH:

Watercress

Sour-Cream–Chive Sauce (recipe follows)

Put the tomatoes and the purée in which they were packed into a large, heavy skillet with the garlic, bay leaf, and cloves. Break up the tomatoes with a metal spoon and bring to a simmer. Cover the pan and cook gently for 30 minutes, stirring occasionally. Purée through a food mill. You should have about 5 cups. Add salt and pepper to taste and the dill and chives.

Soften the gelatin in the cold water and lemon juice, and dissolve over low heat, stirring constantly. Let cool slightly, then stir into the tomato mixture. Pour into a lightly oiled 5- or 6-cup ring mold and chill until set.

To serve, unmold onto a platter and garnish with watercress. Serve with Sour-Cream–Chive Sauce.

6 TO 8 SERVINGS

To Unmold a Mousse or Aspic
Loosen the edges by running a knife all around between the mousse and the container. Place a serving plate on top and, holding both the plate and the mold, invert. Tap lightly on the counter. If the contents do not come out easily, briefly dip the bottom of the mold into a pan of warm water.

SOUR-CREAM–CHIVE SAUCE

¾ cup sour cream
3 tablespoons mayonnaise (Hellman's)
1½ teaspoons Dijon mustard
1½ teaspoons lemon or lime juice
2 teaspoons minced fresh chives

Combine all the ingredients, cover, and chill until serving.

ABOUT 1 CUP

ZUCCHINI CASSEROLE

This recipe comes from our good friend Bill MacDonald. It is lighter and more digestible than similar casseroles in which the vegetables are sautéed in oil before baking.

3 pounds small, firm
zucchini, sliced
¼ inch thick
2 large tomatoes, sliced
1 large onion, sliced very
thin
12 ounces mushrooms,
cleaned and trimmed,
quartered if large

Dill or basil, fresh if
available
Salt
Fresh-ground pepper
⅓ cup fresh-grated
Parmesan cheese or
more, to taste
Approximately 3
tablespoons olive oil

Preheat the oven to 350°. Butter a large, wide casserole.

Place a thick layer of zucchini in the casserole, then add a few slices of tomato, onion, and some of the mushrooms. Sprinkle sparingly with dill or basil, salt and pepper, and grated Parmesan. Continue adding layers in this order, ending with the Parmesan. Drizzle the olive oil on top. Cover loosely with aluminum foil and bake for 30 minutes. Uncover, and bake about 1 hour longer. Liquid will accumulate in the bottom of the casserole, so it is best to serve with a slotted spoon.

6 TO 8 SERVINGS

SALADS

In addition to the salads in this section, see also Parmesan, Mushroom, and Celery Salad, page 17, and Roman-Style Melon, page 18.

ARUGOLA, MUSHROOM, AND ENDIVE SALAD

An especially nice salad to follow a roast or other dinner party entrée.

FOR THE VINAIGRETTE:

> *⅓ cup olive oil*
> *1 tablespoon wine vinegar*
> *1 tablespoon lemon juice*
> *Fresh-ground pepper*
> *1 garlic clove, peeled and cut in half*

FOR THE SALAD:

> *1 large bunch of arugola (4 ounces)*
> *1 Belgian endive*
> *¼ pound mushrooms, cleaned, trimmed, and sliced*

Combine the ingredients for the vinaigrette 1 hour or longer before preparing the salad.

Wash the arugola in a sinkful of water to remove all the sand and dirt, and dry thoroughly. Slice the endive in half lengthwise and then across ¼ inch thick. Combine the arugola, endive, and mushrooms in a salad bowl. Discard the garlic clove and toss the salad and vinaigrette just before serving.

3 TO 4 SERVINGS

To store salad greens, dry well and keep in the refrigerator in a very large plastic bag so that they are not packed or crowded. Or, put them in a colander that has been wrapped in a sheet of wax paper to allow air to circulate.

ENDIVE, SORREL, AND CHIVE SALAD

A delicate salad to serve in early spring.

FOR THE VINAIGRETTE:

⅓ cup olive oil
1 tablespoon plus 1 teaspoon white wine vinegar
1 garlic clove, peeled and cut in half

FOR THE SALAD:

> *3 large Belgian endive*
> *1½ cups sorrel leaves, packed*
> *1½ tablespoons minced chives*
> *Fresh-ground white pepper*

Combine the ingredients for the vinaigrette several hours before serving.

Slice the endive in half lengthwise, then cut them horizontally into inch-long sections. Chop the sorrel coarse. Put the endive, sorrel, chives, and pepper to taste in a salad bowl. Chill until serving. Remove the garlic clove from the vinaigrette and toss the dressing and salad just before serving.

6 SERVINGS

FENNEL AND BASIL SALAD

For this salad, the fennel is steamed and then marinated in oil and vinegar.

> *2 medium-large fennel bulbs, washed and trimmed*
> *3 tablespoons olive oil*
> *2 teaspoons wine vinegar*
> *1 small garlic clove, peeled*
> *1 to 2 tablespoons minced fennel leaves*
> *½ cup chopped fresh basil leaves*
> *Salt*
> *Fresh-ground pepper*

Cut the fennel bulbs in half lengthwise. With the cut side down, slice each half crosswise into ¼-inch strips. Place in a steamer basket over boiling water and cook for a few minutes, covered, until tender but not limp. Mix the oil and vinegar and grate a bit of the garlic into the vinaigrette. Toss with the fennel while it is still warm. Let cool slightly and then mix with the remaining ingredients.

4 SERVINGS

POTATO SALAD

⅔ cup olive oil
¼ cup red wine vinegar
1 small garlic clove, peeled
    and pressed
3 pounds red-skinned
    potatoes
⅔ cup very thin-sliced
    red onions

½ cup minced fresh
    parsley
Fresh-ground pepper
1 cup mayonnaise
1 tablespoon
    Düsseldorf or
    Dijon mustard

Combine the oil, vinegar, and garlic and reserve.

Cook the potatoes in boiling water to cover until tender. Drain, peel, and slice them ¼ inch thick. While the potatoes are still warm, toss them with the oil and vinegar mixture. Let cool to room temperature, then add the onions, parsley, and pepper. Combine the mayonnaise and mustard and fold into the salad. Refrigerate until serving.

6 TO 8 SERVINGS

RICE SALAD WITH TOMATOES AND FRESH HERBS

This is a good side dish to serve with a light summer entrée, particularly fish or chicken. The rice is marinated in a lemon vinaigrette and combined with fresh basil, parsley, pine nuts, and tomatoes.

FOR THE VINAIGRETTE:

½ cup olive oil
3 tablespoons lemon juice
1 garlic clove, peeled and cut in half

FOR THE SALAD:

1⅔ cups rice
Salt
1 cup chopped fresh basil leaves
⅓ cup minced fresh parsley
Grated zest of 2 medium-size lemons
½ cup pine nuts
1 pint cherry tomatoes, cut in half
Fresh-ground pepper

Combine the ingredients for the vinaigrette at least 1 hour before preparing the salad.

Bring a very large pot of water to a boil. Add salt and the rice and cook for 17 minutes, or until tender but slightly firm. Turn the rice into a colander, rinse under hot tap water, and drain well. Put the rice into a mixing bowl and toss with the vinaigrette while it is still hot, discarding the garlic clove. Let cool to room temperature before adding the remaining ingredients. Season to taste. If the rice seems dry, add a bit more oil and lemon juice. Serve either chilled or at room temperature.

NOTE: If you are serving this salad in the evening, it is best to make it early in the day to allow time for the flavor of the basil to develop fully.

8 TO 10 SERVINGS

SLICED AVOCADO AND CANTALOUPE

However unlikely this combination may sound, it is a delicious and refreshing one (provided the avocado and cantaloupe are at their peak). It was suggested to me by our friend Jill Stallworthy.

3 tablespoons olive oil
1 tablespoon lemon juice
½ cantaloupe
2 large avocados
Salt
Fresh-ground pepper

Combine the oil and lemon juice. Remove the rind from the cantaloupe and slice lengthwise, ½ inch thick. Shortly before serving, peel the avocados. Cut them in half, remove the pits, and slice lengthwise into ½-inch-thick strips. Pour about half the vinaigrette into a shallow bowl and dip in each slice of avocado to prevent discoloration. Alternate the avocado slices on individual salad plates with slices of cantaloupe and drizzle the remaining vinaigrette over all. Cover with plastic wrap and refrigerate. Season with salt and pepper just before serving.

6 TO 8 SERVINGS

SPINACH, AVOCADO, AND RED PEPPER SALAD

2-87
excellent
used basic
Fennel dressing
very good!

One 10-ounce package fresh spinach
1 sweet red pepper
1 large avocado
bacon, cooked + crumbled

FOR THE VINAIGRETTE:

2 tablespoons plus 2 teaspoons white wine vinegar
2 teaspoons Dijon mustard
1 tablespoon mayonnaise
1 tiny garlic clove (corn-kernel size), pressed
⅔ cup olive oil

Wash the spinach in a sinkful of water, discarding the stems and any wilted leaves. Drain, dry well, and tear into bite-size pieces. Core and seed the pepper and cut into ¼-inch strips. Put the spinach and pepper into a salad bowl. Peel and cut up the avocado just before serving and add it to the salad.

To make the dressing: Combine the vinegar with the mustard, mayonnaise, and garlic, whisking to blend, then add the oil. Toss with the salad and serve immediately.

4 TO 6 SERVINGS

TOMATO, PEACH, AND RED ONION SALAD

This is a delicious and novel combination, but only for mid to late summer, when peaches and tomatoes are at their peak. The salad is easy to make, but should not be prepared more than a half hour before serving.

FOR THE VINAIGRETTE:

¼ cup olive oil
1½ tablespoons white wine vinegar
1 garlic clove, peeled and cut in half

FOR THE SALAD:

2 large ripe tomatoes
2 large ripe peaches
½ medium-size red onion, peeled and sliced thin
½ cup chopped fresh basil or mint leaves
Salt
Fresh-ground pepper

Combine the ingredients for the vinaigrette an hour or more before serving.

Shortly before serving, immerse the tomatoes and peaches, one at a time, in boiling water for about 20 seconds to loosen their skins. Peel and slice them. If the tomatoes are very juicy, drain them on paper towels. Combine the tomatoes and peaches in a salad bowl with the red onion, basil or mint, and seasoning to taste. Discard the garlic clove and gently toss the vinaigrette with the salad.

4 SERVINGS

TOMATO SALAD PROVENÇALE

Sliced tomatoes with a piquant dressing combining anchovies, capers, onion, and parsley in a vinaigrette.

FOR THE DRESSING:

> *1 very small garlic clove, peeled and grated or pressed*
> *2 anchovy fillets, minced*
> *1 tablespoon capers, well drained and chopped or slightly*
>   *crushed*
> *3 tablespoons minced red onion*
> *1 tablespoon minced fresh parsley*
> *¼ cup olive oil*
> *1 tablespoon wine vinegar*
>
> *2 medium-size tomatoes or 1 extra-large*
> *Salt*
> *Fresh-ground pepper*

Combine the ingredients for the dressing and reserve.

Shortly before serving, immerse the tomatoes in boiling water for about 20 seconds to loosen their skins. Peel and slice them. Season with salt and pepper and spoon the dressing over each slice.

2 TO 3 SERVINGS

WATERCRESS AND MUSHROOM SALAD

This salad should be made only with large-leaved, dark green bunches of watercress, not the hothouse variety. It is dressed in a piquant, slightly creamy, mustard vinaigrette.

FOR THE DRESSING:

>   *2 tablespoons wine vinegar*
>   *1 tablespoon Düsseldorf mustard*
>   *1 tablespoon mayonnaise*
>   *½ cup olive oil*
>   *1 garlic clove, peeled*

FOR THE SALAD:

>   *1 extra-large or 2 medium-size bunches of watercress*
>   *(5 ounces)*
>   *4 ounces firm, white mushrooms*

Whisk together the vinegar, mustard, and mayonnaise until smooth, then add the oil. Grate in a little of the garlic clove.

Rinse and dry the watercress. Stack evenly and slice across into roughly 2-inch lengths. Clean, trim, and slice the mushrooms and put them into a salad bowl with the watercress. Just before serving, whisk or shake the dressing to homogenize, then toss with the salad.

3 TO 4 SERVINGS

WHITE BEAN SALAD

Other fresh herbs, such as basil, cilantro, tarragon, or marjoram, may be substituted for those suggested below. Add them according to taste, as they vary in strength. If parsley is the only fresh herb available, use a little more of it and add just a little dried dill or basil.

FOR THE VINAIGRETTE:

> ½ *cup olive oil*
> 2 *tablespoons lemon juice*
> 2 *tablespoons wine vinegar*
> 1 *garlic clove, peeled and cut in half*

FOR THE SALAD:

> 1 *cup (8 ounces) dried white beans, such as Great Northern, soaked overnight in 2 quarts water*
> *A few parsley sprigs*
> *A few celery leaves*
> 1 *small onion, peeled*
> 2 *tablespoons lemon juice*
> *Salt*
> *Fresh-ground pepper*
> 2 *tablespoons minced fresh parsley*

> 2 *to 3 tablespoons minced fresh mint leaves*
> 1 ½ *tablespoons minced fresh dill*
> ⅓ *to* ½ *cup chopped sweet red pepper*
> 3 *tablespoons fine-chopped red onion*
> 1 *scant cup cherry tomatoes, cut in half*

Combine the ingredients for the vinaigrette and reserve.

To boil the beans: Add the parsley sprigs, celery leaves, onion, and lemon juice to the soaking water. Make sure there is plenty of water to cover the beans, and bring to a simmer, partially covered. Continue cooking, at a simmer, for 1 to 1½ hours, or until the beans are quite tender but not falling apart. Drain well in a colander and discard the parsley and celery leaves and the onion.

Turn the beans into a salad bowl and toss with the vinaigrette (discarding the garlic), and salt and pepper while they are still warm. Let cool to room temperature, then add the herbs, red pepper, red onion, and tomatoes.

NOTE: The beans have a great capacity for absorbing the vinaigrette, and if they have been prepared several hours before serving, they may become dry. If so, stir in about 2 tablespoons olive oil and 1 tablespoon vinegar or lemon juice just before serving.

6 SERVINGS

Breads

A homemade bread adds a special touch to a simple meal, and it need not involve a lot of work. This chapter includes a variety of breads, appropriate to different menus, but all are characterized by ease of preparation. The traditional method of making yeast bread is simplified in recipes that require no kneading and only one rising. In working out a biscuit recipe, I have found that the biscuits can be made in advance up to the actual baking and held in the refrigerator, so that one need not be immersed in butter and flour in the midst of a party. Other recipes include a number of quick breads, such as Bacon-Corn Bread and Miniature Lime Muffins, that can be made ahead and reheated before serving. The chapter concludes with some appetizing ways to prepare store-bought bread as substantial accompaniments to an entrée.

HOMEMADE BREADS

BACON-CORN BREAD

A light and moist cornbread with a crisp topping of crumbled bacon.

¼ pound bacon (4 to 5 slices)
1 cup flour
2 tablespoons sugar
½ teaspoon salt
½ teaspoon baking soda

1 ½ teaspoons baking powder
1 cup yellow cornmeal
1 egg
1 cup buttermilk

Broil or fry the bacon until crisp. Reserve ¼ cup of the rendered fat. Drain the bacon on paper towels and crumble.

Preheat the oven to 425°. Butter and flour an 8- or 9-inch square pan.

Sift together the flour, sugar, salt, baking soda, and baking powder into a mixing bowl. Stir in the cornmeal. Beat the egg lightly with the buttermilk and stir into the dry mixture with the reserved bacon fat. Turn into the prepared pan and scatter the crumbled bacon over the top. Bake for about 20 minutes, or until a toothpick tests clean. Serve warm, with unsalted butter.

6 SERVINGS

Cooking Bacon

Since I learned this method, I no longer fry bacon. It can be cooked perfectly under the broiler without spattering the stove top and the cook and without dirtying a skillet. If possible, adjust the shelf to 7 or 9 inches below the broiling unit. If the shelf cannot be adjusted, lower the heat so that the bacon will not char. Put the bacon in a single layer in a shallow pan (an aluminum foil one will do). Turn the bacon over once during cooking and drain the fat from the pan once or twice. The bacon will be cooked in 5 minutes or less. Watch it carefully so the edges don't burn. When cooked, drain on paper towels.

BLUEBERRY DROP BISCUITS

These light, flaky biscuits can be made rather quickly because the dough is not rolled out and cut, but dropped from a spoon. They can be served for breakfast, tea, or even with a light salad lunch.

2 cups flour
¼ cup sugar
¼ teaspoon salt
1 ½ teaspoons baking powder
½ teaspoon baking soda
¼ pound (1 stick) unsalted butter, well chilled and cut into bits

1 cup blueberries, rinsed and dried
Approximately 1 cup buttermilk
1 to 2 teaspoons sugar mixed with a little ground cinnamon

Preheat the oven to 400°. Butter a large cookie sheet.

Combine the flour, sugar, salt, baking powder, and baking soda in a large mixing bowl. With the tips of your fingers, rub in the butter to break it down into small flakes. Gently fold in the blueberries. Gradually stir in the buttermilk, adding just enough to make a very moist, but not runny, dough. Drop by heaping tablespoonsful onto the cookie sheet, about 2 inches apart. Sprinkle the tops with the cinnamon-sugar. Bake for 12 to 15 minutes, or until the biscuits are lightly browned and a metal skewer tests clean. Serve warm.

15 BISCUITS

NOTE: To make plain drop biscuits, follow the recipe above, but omit the blueberries and the cinnamon-sugar topping. Use 1½ tablespoons sugar, ½ teaspoon salt, and ⅞ cup buttermilk.

Measure dry ingredients, such as sugar and flour, with stainless-steel dry-measure cups, which can be leveled off at the rim with the blade of a knife to give accurate measurements. A set includes measures for 1/8, 1/4, 1/3, 1/2, and 1 cup. Pyrex measuring cups with a lip for pouring should be used to measure liquid ingredients only.

BUTTERMILK BISCUITS

Freshly baked biscuits are a delicious addition to a meal, but I used to be reluctant to make them because of the last-minute work involved. They are just not as good reheated. I have since discovered that they can be prepared ahead up to the actual baking, vastly simplifying the dinner preparation.

2 cups flour
2 teaspoons sugar
1 1/2 teaspoons baking powder
1/2 teaspoon baking soda
1/2 teaspoon salt
6 tablespoons cold, unsalted butter, cut into small pieces
1 tablespoon cold vegetable shortening
Approximately 3/4 cup buttermilk

Preheat the oven to 400°.

Sift the flour with the sugar, baking powder, baking soda, and salt into a large mixing bowl. With the tips of your fingers, rub in the butter and shortening until the mixture resembles coarse meal. Stir in enough buttermilk, mixing with your hands as the dough stiffens, to make a soft dough that is not too sticky. Knead 1 or 2 turns on a lightly floured board and roll out to a thickness of ½ inch. Cut into 2-inch rounds with a floured biscuit cutter or the rim of a glass. (Press the biscuit cutter straight down and lift it up without twisting, so that you do not seal the edges.) Place the biscuits about an inch apart on an ungreased baking sheet. (The biscuits may be made ahead to this point. Cover the baking sheet airtight with plastic wrap. If they are to be baked in 1 or 2 hours, store at room temperature; otherwise refrigerate. Be sure to return the biscuits to room temperature well before baking or they will not rise properly.)

Brush the tops of the biscuits with a little milk if a sheen is desired, and bake for 10 minutes, or until they are lightly browned. Wrap in foil and serve immediately.

12 BISCUITS

Quick breads, muffins, and cakes will rise higher and be lighter if all the ingredients are at room temperature or slightly warmed before mixing and baking. Uncracked eggs can be warmed in a bowl of hot tap water.

CORN MUFFINS

---

1 cup flour	*1 egg*
2½ tablespoons sugar	*1 cup sour cream*
¾ teaspoon salt	*6 tablespoons (¾*
½ teaspoon baking soda	*stick) unsalted*
2 teaspoons baking powder	*butter, melted*
1 cup yellow cornmeal	

Preheat the oven to 425°. Generously butter a set of twelve muffin tins.

Sift the flour, sugar, salt, baking soda, and baking powder into a mixing bowl. Stir in the cornmeal. Beat the egg in a separate bowl and stir in the sour cream. Add this to the flour mixture with the melted butter, stirring only until combined. The batter should be lumpy. Fill the prepared muffin tins to three-quarter capacity and bake for about 15 minutes, or until the muffins are lightly browned and a toothpick tests clean. Serve warm, with unsalted butter. (If baking ahead, reheat the muffins, tightly wrapped in foil, for 10 minutes, in an oven preheated to 350°.)

12 MUFFINS

EASY CHEDDAR BREAD

Although this is a yeast bread, it is not difficult to make, as it requires almost no kneading and only one rising. Each slice is spiraled with a band of Cheddar cheese. Serve it reheated in foil in the oven or toasted and buttered.

> *½ pound medium-sharp Cheddar cheese*
> *3 cups flour*
> *1 package active dry yeast*
> *1 teaspoon sugar*
> *¼ cup warm water*
> *¾ teaspoon salt*
> *Approximately ⅔ cup additional water*

Butter and flour an 8-by-5-inch loaf pan. Grate the cheese in a food processor with 2 tablespoons of the flour. Stir the yeast and sugar into the warm water and let stand until the mixture bubbles up. Mix the rest of the flour with the salt in a large mixing bowl. Stir in the yeast mixture and just enough additional water to make a firm but somewhat moist dough, mixing with your hands as the dough becomes stiff. Mix half the grated cheese (about 1 cup) into the dough, kneading it a few times to incorporate thoroughly. On a floured board, roll the dough into a rectangle about 8 by 12 inches. Sprinkle the rest of the grated cheese evenly over the surface. Roll the dough up from the short end, pinching the edges to seal. Place, seam side down, in the prepared pan. Lightly oil the surface of the loaf and cover with plastic wrap. Put it in a warm place to rise until doubled in volume. (The loaf should just crest above the rim of the pan.)

Preheat the oven to 375°. Bake the bread for 35 to 40 minutes, or until a skewer tests clean. Turn out of the pan and return to the oven for 3 to 5 minutes to brown the bottom and sides lightly. Let cool on a wire rack and reheat, wrapped in foil, or toast the bread before serving.

1 LOAF

On Baking Yeast Breads

Dissolving Yeast: The most reliable way to activate yeast is to stir it into a little warm water. The water temperature should be between 105° and 115°— warmer than body temperature but not scalding. Use hot tap water and, if you are inexperienced, gauge the temperature with a candy thermometer. If you add a little sugar to the water (½ teaspoon is enough), the mixture will bubble up after a few minutes, proving that the yeast is active.

Rub your hands with vegetable oil before kneading or mixing bread to keep the dough from sticking to them.

If you don't have a warm place for dough to rise, heat the oven very slightly, then turn it off before putting the dough in. Or put the bowl or pan containing the dough on a wire rack set over a bowl of warm water.

EASY SOUR CREAM BREAD

If you are not in the habit of making yeast breads, this is a good one to start with. As in the preceding recipe for Easy Cheddar Bread, a minimum of time and work is required—very little kneading and only one rising. The bread is, nevertheless, very moist and light, with a lovely homemade flavor.

1/4 cup warm water
1 package active dry yeast
1 teaspoon sugar
Approximately 2 1/2 cups flour
1 teaspoon salt
1/4 teaspoon baking soda
1 cup sour cream, or 1/2 cup sour cream and 1/2 cup milk
*   or small-curd cottage cheese*

Butter and flour an 8-by-5-inch loaf pan. Run the tap water until it is hot but not scalding (about 105°). Put the warm water into a Pyrex measure, stir in the yeast and sugar, and wait for the mixture to bubble up.

In a large mixing bowl, stir together 2 1/4 cups of the flour, the salt, and the baking soda. Stir in the yeast mixture and then the sour cream (or sour cream mixture). Mix with your hands and gradually add enough of the remaining flour to make a moist but firm dough. (Note: If using part milk, you may need extra flour to make a firm dough.) Roll or pat it into a log about 8 inches long and put it into the prepared loaf pan. Lightly oil the surface of the dough and cover the pan with plastic wrap. Put it in a warm place to rise until the loaf just reaches the rim of the pan—about 1 hour.

Preheat the oven to 375°. Bake the bread for 35 to 40 minutes, or until a skewer tests clean. Turn out of the pan and let cool on a wire rack for several minutes before slicing. Or let cool completely and reheat, wrapped in foil, before serving. This bread is also good toasted and buttered.

I LOAF

MINIATURE LIME MUFFINS

Serve a basket of these muffins with Chicken Salad with Creamy Herb Dressing (page 125) or for afternoon tea.

> 6 tablespoons unsalted butter, softened
> ⅞ cup sugar
> Grated zest of 3 limes
> 2 eggs
> 1½ cups flour
> 1½ teaspoons baking powder
> ¼ teaspoon salt
> ⅔ cup milk

Preheat the oven to 350°. Butter and flour three sets of miniature muffin tins (or bake the muffins in 3 batches).

Cream the butter with an electric mixer, gradually adding the sugar. Add the lime zest and the eggs and beat until light. Sift the flour with the baking powder and salt and add it to the batter alternately with the milk, beginning and ending with the flour mixture. Fill the muffin tins almost to the top with the batter. Bake for 15 minutes, or until a toothpick tests clean. Loosen carefully and serve warm. Or let cool on a wire rack and reheat, tightly wrapped in foil, before serving.

2½ TO 3 DOZEN MINIATURE MUFFINS

POPOVERS

Popovers were a popular choice for Sunday dinner when I was young, and my mother was adept at making them. They always puffed up miraculously; indeed, almost popping out of the pan. Since few people serve them anymore (few people serve Sunday dinner, either), I include this recipe as a reminder. Popovers are quickly and easily made and can add a special touch to a meal.

> *2 eggs*
> *1 cup milk*
> *1 cup flour*
> *¼ teaspoon salt*
> *1 tablespoon unsalted butter, melted*

Before you begin to mix the batter, preheat the oven to 450°, as the popovers must be baked as soon as the batter is blended.

Butter a set of twelve deep muffin or popover tins. In a large mixing bowl, beat the eggs with an electric mixer, gradually adding first the milk, then the flour and salt, then the butter. The mixture should be thin. Pour immediately into the prepared tins, filling to two-thirds capacity. Bake for 15 minutes. Reduce the oven temperature to 350° and bake 15 minutes longer, or until the popovers are puffed up and crisp and well browned. Loosen from the pan with the blade of a knife. Pierce the bottom of each to allow the steam to escape and serve immediately.

12 POPOVERS

QUICK WALNUT BREAD

This is very much like a soda bread, but made with whole milk rather than buttermilk. It has a flaky, biscuitlike texture and is best served hot from the oven. It goes well with entrée soups, stews, and roast chicken.

2 cups flour
½ teaspoon baking soda
½ teaspoon cream of tartar
1 scant teaspoon sugar
¼ teaspoon salt
½ cup coarse-chopped walnuts
3 tablespoons unsalted butter, well chilled and cut
into bits
½ cup milk

Preheat the oven to 375°. Lightly butter a baking sheet or pie tin.

Mix the dry ingredients and walnuts in a large mixing bowl. Rub in the butter with the tips of your fingers. Gradually add enough milk to make a firm but moist dough, mixing with your hands as the dough becomes stiff. Shape into a round loaf, about 6 inches in diameter, and place on the prepared pan. With a sharp knife, cut an X across the surface of the loaf about ¼ inch deep. Bake for 25 minutes, or just until the top is lightly browned and a skewer tests clean. Serve immediately with unsalted butter. Or let cool on a wire rack and reheat, wrapped in foil, before serving.

1 ROUND LOAF, OR 4 GENEROUS SERVINGS

SCONES

When we have house guests, I serve these scones for breakfast, along with a bowl of strawberries or citrus fruit. They are especially good with unsalted butter and honey.

> *2 cups flour*
> *2 tablespoons sugar*
> *1 teaspoon baking powder*
> *¼ teaspoon baking soda*
> *¼ pound (1 stick) unsalted butter, well chilled and cut*
>   *into bits*
> *⅔ cup sour cream*

FOR THE GLAZE:

> *Cream or whole milk*
> *2 teaspoons sugar mixed with a little ground cinnamon*

Preheat the oven to 400°. Lightly butter a baking sheet.

Sift the flour, sugar, baking powder, and baking soda into a mixing bowl. With the tips of your fingers, lightly rub the butter into the flour mixture, breaking the butter down into small bits. Stir in just enough sour cream to make a soft but not sticky dough. Mix with your hands as the dough stiffens, and do not overwork it. Put the dough on a lightly floured board and gently pat it into a circle about 7 inches in diameter and ¾ inch thick. Divide it into eight wedges, cutting straight down with a sharp knife. (Do not saw.) Brush the top of each wedge with a little cream or milk and sprinkle with the cinnamon-sugar.* Place the wedges about 1 inch apart on the baking sheet. Bake for 15 minutes, or just until cooked through and lightly browned.

8 SCONES

* When serving these with a lunch or dinner entrée, omit the cinnamon-sugar topping.

RECIPES USING
STORE-BOUGHT BREADS

BAGUETTES WITH MELTED BRIE

This is a particularly good accompaniment to Onion and Mushroom Soup (page 48), as well as steaks, chicken, and chops.

Cut French baguettes in half lengthwise and cut each half into 4-inch lengths. Spread with a thick layer of Brie* and toast under the broiler until the cheese has melted.

 * Other cheeses, such as mozzarella, Jarlsberg, or chèvre, may be substituted.

HERB AND PARMESAN BREAD

 1 loaf French or Italian bread
 3 to 4 tablespoons unsalted butter
 1 garlic clove, peeled and crushed
 Dried basil
 Dried rosemary, crushed
 Approximately ½ cup fresh-grated Parmesan cheese

Cut the bread in half lengthwise. Melt the butter with the garlic. Discard the garlic clove and brush the butter over the cut sides of the bread. Sprinkle with a very small amount of basil and rosemary. Cut each half loaf into 3-inch lengths. Reassemble the loaf and wrap in foil.

Preheat the oven to 350°. Heat the bread for 15 to 20 minutes. Open the foil, lay the bread on top, cut sides up, and sprinkle generously with grated Parmesan. Place under the broiler for a few seconds to melt the cheese. Watch carefully so that it doesn't burn.

4 TO 6 SERVINGS

ITALIAN BREAD WITH ROAST PEPPERS, MUSHROOMS, AND OLIVES

This recipe was inspired by a photograph in *W*—a slice of Italian bread with a roast pepper mixture on top. It looked delicious and easy, and struck me as the perfect accompaniment to a bowl of steamed mussels or any simple fish soup.

4 large sweet peppers, preferably red or yellow, or both
3 ounces mushrooms, cleaned, trimmed, and cut in half
10 to 12 Calamata olives, cut in half and pitted
¼ cup olive oil
1 garlic clove, cut in half
1 tablespoon well-drained capers
Minced fresh parsley or basil
A loaf of good, firm Italian bread

Place the peppers on a baking sheet under the broiler about 2 inches from the heat. Roast, turning the peppers as the skins blister and darken, until charred on all sides. This will take 10 to 15 minutes. Peel under cold running water. Remove the stems and seeds and cut into 2-inch-wide strips. Drain in a colander and pat dry with paper towels.

Put the peppers in a shallow bowl with the mushrooms, olives, oil, garlic, capers, and parsley or basil and allow to marinate for several hours, stirring occasionally.

Discard the garlic before serving. Put a basket of Italian bread, sliced about ½ inch thick, on the table and allow each guest to assemble his own open-faced sandwich. (If you assemble the sandwiches in the kitchen, do so just before serving.)

4 SERVINGS

MIDDLE EASTERN BREAD

Various forms of Middle Eastern bread are widely available, usually called pita bread, Sahara bread, or Syrian bread. My favorite, however, is known as Marouk and is a bit harder to find. While all are flat breads, Marouk is much thinner than the others and comes in very large flat rounds, usually folded over into quarters. It should be buttered lightly, cut into small wedges, and toasted under the broiler. It will take less than a minute to turn golden and must be watched carefully or it will burn. It can be served hot out of the oven, but will also stay crisp at room temperature if stored airtight.

This bread makes a good snack to serve with drinks or an excellent accompaniment to soups, composed salads, or almost any entrée. It can be varied by sprinkling with grated Parmesan, sesame seeds, or just a little dill or lemon-pepper marinade before toasting.

OPEN-FACE CUCUMBER SANDWICHES

4 slices very thin-sliced whole wheat or whole-grain bread
Mayonnaise
Sour cream
Fresh dill, mint, or parsley, minced
1 cucumber, peeled and sliced thin

Cut each slice of bread in half diagonally. Mix 3 parts mayonnaise to 1 part sour cream and add a little dill, mint, or parsley. Spread on the bread triangles and top with cucumber slices.

8 TRIANGLES

Desserts

FRESH fruit is an important staple of simple cuisine, and the desserts that follow depend heavily on its use. There are pies for every season—Warm Pear-Amaretto Pie or Apple Crisp for fall and winter; Blueberry Cobbler, Deep-Dish Peach Pie, and Peach-Brandy Pie for summer; as well as some quick and light fruit desserts, such as Raspberry-Cassis Fool and Fluffy Lime Mousse. In addition, I have appended a list of Simple Fresh Fruit Desserts, offering several easy serving suggestions.

The second section of this chapter offers a few recipes for cakes and cookies. They are not elaborate or difficult to make, but I think they are very good and are perhaps more welcome at the end of a meal than fancier, tiered confections.

The final section deals with frozen desserts. I have a weakness for ice cream, but not for kitchen machinery, and therefore go out of my way to devise ice cream formulas that do not require special equipment. The recipes included here use various methods to produce frozen desserts that are smooth and creamy without the icy texture characteristic of many homemade ice creams. They are easily prepared and then simply left in the freezing compartment of the refrigerator to become firm.

PIES AND FRUIT DESSERTS

APPLE CRISP

¼ *cup dried currants*
¼ *cup applejack or brandy*
3½ *pounds McIntosh apples*
2 *tablespoons lemon juice*
2 *tablespoons brown sugar*
½ *teaspoon ground cinnamon*

FOR THE CRUMB TOPPING:

6 *tablespoons (¾ stick) unsalted butter, cut up*
⅔ *cup chopped pecans*
¾ *cup flour*
½ *cup brown sugar, packed*
½ *teaspoon ground cinnamon*

1 *cup heavy cream whipped with 2 teaspoons sugar, ½*
  teaspoon vanilla, and 1 tablespoon applejack or
  brandy
Or vanilla ice cream

Put the currants and applejack or brandy into a small saucepan and simmer gently until the moisture is absorbed.

Peel, core, and slice the apples ¼ inch thick. As they are peeled, toss them with the lemon juice in a large bowl. Add the brown sugar and the cinnamon and currants and mix well. Turn them into a buttered 2-quart casserole, pressing down firmly. Put the ingredients for the crumb topping into a mixing bowl and mix with your fingers until the butter is incorporated and the topping is crumbly and cohesive. Cover the apples with the crumb mixture.

Preheat the oven to 350°. Bake for 30 to 35 minutes, or until the apples are tender but not too soft. Serve warm, with whipped cream or vanilla ice cream.

NOTE: The apple crisp may be made in advance and reheated before serving for 15 to 20 minutes at 325°.

8 SERVINGS

BLUEBERRY COBBLER

FOR THE PIECRUST:

> 2 ¼ cups flour
> Grated zest of 1 large lemon
> 3 ½ tablespoons sugar
> ⅛ teaspoon salt
> ¼ pound (1 stick) unsalted butter, well chilled and cut
>   into small bits
> ¼ cup cold vegetable shortening
> Approximately ¼ cup cold water

FOR THE FILLING:

> 2 *pints blueberries, rinsed and dried*
> 6 *tablespoons flour (less if the berries seem dry)*
> ¾ *cup sugar*
> 3 *tablespoons unsalted butter, melted*
>
> 2 *teaspoons sugar mixed with a large pinch of ground*
>   *cinnamon*
> *Vanilla ice cream*

Either make the piecrust in a food processor according to the method described on page 208; or combine the flour, lemon zest, sugar, and salt in a large mixing bowl and rub in the butter and shortening with the tips of your fingers. Add just enough water to form a dough, cover with wax paper, and refrigerate until firm (30 minutes or longer).

Preheat the oven to 400°.

Roll out the dough between two sheets of floured wax paper into a very large circle (about 14 inches in diameter) to line a deep 6-cup baking dish and overlap at the sides. Remove one sheet of wax paper and carefully fit the pastry into the dish, peeling off the other sheet of wax paper as you do so. Patch any holes or tears by pressing scraps of dough over them. (It doesn't matter if it looks messy.) In a mixing bowl, gently toss the blueberries with the flour and sugar, then mix in the melted butter. Turn into the baking dish. Fold over the overlapping sides of the piecrust to cover the top, patching to cover the surface completely. With the point of a knife, make several vents for steam and sprinkle the crust with the cinnamon-sugar. Bake for about 30 minutes, or until the crust is lightly browned. Let cool to room temperature on a wire rack. Serve with vanilla ice cream.

6 SERVINGS

Preparing Pie Dough

Good pastry can be made in a food processor if you are careful not to over-process it. Put the dry ingredients into the work bowl and add cold butter (cut into small pieces) and/or cold shortening. Process, pulsing off and on, until the fat is broken down into small bits. With the motor running, add the cold liquid in a thin stream, but (contrary to what the instruction book tells you) do not wait for the dough to form a ball. Before it begins to cohere, turn off the motor and turn the dough onto a sheet of wax paper. With your hands, push it into a ball and knead once or twice to make sure it holds together. Wrap in wax paper and refrigerate until it is firm enough to roll out (30 minutes or longer). The easiest way to roll out pastry is between two lightly floured sheets of wax paper. When it is the proper size, peel off the top sheet, invert the dough into the pie plate, then peel off the other sheet.

DEEP-DISH PEACH PIE

FOR THE PIECRUST:

1½ cups flour
Grated zest of 1 lemon
3 tablespoons sugar
⅛ teaspoon salt
6 tablespoons unsalted butter, well chilled and cut into
   small bits
3 tablespoons vegetable shortening, well chilled
Approximately 3 tablespoons cold water

FOR THE FILLING:

3 pounds peaches, peeled and sliced ⅜ inch thick
1 cup plus 2 tablespoons sugar
6 tablespoons flour*
4 tablespoons (½ stick) unsalted butter, melted
3 tablespoons medium-dry sherry

Cream or milk
Sugar

Vanilla ice cream

* Use a little more flour if the peaches are especially juicy.

To make the piecrust: Combine the ingredients in a food processor
according to the instructions on page 208. Or mix the flour, lemon
zest, sugar, and salt in a large bowl and rub in the butter and shortening with the tips of your fingers. Add just enough water to form a

dough, cover with wax paper, and refrigerate until firm enough to roll out (30 minutes or longer).

Preheat the oven to 400°.

Toss the peaches with the sugar and flour. Add the melted butter and sherry and mix well. Turn into a pie dish that is about 2 inches deep. (I use a deep Pyrex pie dish that is of 6-cup capacity and 10 inches in diameter at the top, allowing for a large crust.) Roll out the dough between two sheets of lightly floured wax paper into a large circle and place over the pie dish, doubling the edges at the rim and fluting to seal. Brush the surface of the dough with cream or milk and sprinkle lightly with granulated sugar. Bake for 25 minutes, or just until the crust is lightly browned and the peaches are tender. Place on a wire rack and let cool to room temperature before serving. (You may serve the pie warm, but the filling will be more runny. In either case, it is best to serve it in dessert bowls rather than on flat plates.) Accompany with vanilla ice cream.

6 TO 8 SERVINGS

Tomatoes and peaches can be peeled easily if immersed in boiling water for 20 to 30 seconds.

FLUFFY LIME MOUSSE

I've omitted the egg yolks found in most recipes and used only enough gelatin to bind the mixture. The result is a light and airy version of a lime mousse. Be sure to use very fresh limes (smooth, taut rind, no discoloration) or they may have a slightly bitter taste.

> 1½ teaspoons unflavored gelatin
> ¼ cup cold water
> 2 egg whites
> 1 cup heavy cream
> ½ cup plus 1 tablespoon sugar
> ½ teaspoon vanilla extract
> ¼ cup plus 3 tablespoons strained fresh lime juice
> Grated zest of 1 lime

FOR THE TOPPING:

> 1½ cups raspberries, blueberries, or sliced strawberries,
>   sweetened to taste

Soften the gelatin in the cold water and dissolve over low heat, stirring constantly. Remove from the heat and let stand while you beat the egg whites and cream.

Beat the egg whites until they hold soft peaks. Continue beating while gradually adding ½ cup of the sugar. Do not overbeat—they should be moist and not too stiff.

Whip the cream with the vanilla and the remaining tablespoon sugar until it holds soft peaks. Continue beating while gradually adding the dissolved gelatin in a thin stream. Fold the lime juice and zest into the whipped cream, then fold in the egg whites. Turn into a serving bowl, cover with plastic wrap, and chill until firm. Serve with a large spoonful of berries over each portion.

4 SERVINGS

How to Melt Gelatin
The easiest way to melt gelatin is in a stainless-steel measuring cup. Use ¼ cup of cold water or other clear liquid for every envelope of gelatin. Place over low heat and stir until all the granules have dissolved. If you put the cup on top of a simmer pad or "flame tamer" and keep the heat low, it will not be necessary to stir the gelatin, as the pad will keep it from burning. Such a pad is also useful when melting chocolate.

PEACH-BRANDY PIE

This pie is also good made with marsala instead of brandy.

FOR THE PIECRUST:

> *2 cups flour*
> *¼ cup sugar*
> *⅛ teaspoon salt*
> *Grated zest of 1 large lemon*
> *6 tablespoons (¾ stick) unsalted butter, well chilled*
>   *and cut into small bits*
> *5 tablespoons vegetable shortening, well chilled*
> *¼ cup cold water*

FOR THE FILLING:

> *⅓ cup brandy*
> *2 tablespoons cornstarch*
> *2 eggs*
> *1 cup sugar*
> *1 teaspoon vanilla extract*
> *3 tablespoons unsalted butter, melted*
> *1⅓ pounds peaches (5 to 6)*

FOR THE GLAZE:

> *Milk*
> *Sugar*

FOR THE TOPPING:

> *1 cup heavy cream*
> *1 tablespoon brandy*
> *½ teaspoon vanilla extract*
> *2 teaspoons sugar*

Make the pie dough in a food processor according to the instructions on page 208. Or combine the flour, sugar, salt, and lemon zest in a large mixing bowl and rub in the butter and shortening with the tips of your fingers. Add the water, form into a dough, cover with wax paper, and refrigerate until firm enough to roll out (30 minutes or longer).

To make the filling: Mix the brandy with the cornstarch, stirring to dissolve. Lightly beat the eggs in a large mixing bowl and stir in the brandy mixture, the sugar, vanilla, and melted butter. Immerse the peaches in boiling water for 20 or 30 seconds. Peel and slice them into the custard.

Preheat the oven to 350°.

Roll out two-thirds of the dough between two lightly floured sheets of wax paper and fit into a 9-inch pie plate, doubling and fluting the edges. Roll the remaining dough into a rectangle and cut into ten strips, each about ½ inch wide. Pour the filling into the pie shell and lay the strips in a lattice pattern over the top, sealing at the edges. Brush the lattice and fluted edge of the shell with milk and sprinkle with a little sugar. Bake for 45 to 50 minutes, or until the custard is set. (If the edges brown too quickly, cover with a collar of aluminum foil.) Serve the pie warm. If you make it ahead, let cool on a wire rack and reheat, loosely covered with foil, in a 325° oven for 10 to 15 minutes.

To make the topping: Lightly whip the cream with the brandy, vanilla, and sugar. Top each serving with a large spoonful of cream.

6 TO 8 SERVINGS

PEAR AND ALMOND CRUMBLE

This is a good fall and winter dessert. It is made much like an apple crisp, but baked in a shallow pan, with chopped almonds added to the crumb topping. It is especially good served slightly warm, with vanilla ice cream.

> *3½ pounds pears*
> *1 tablespoon lemon juice*

FOR THE TOPPING:

> *⅔ cup chopped almonds**
> *¾ cup flour*
> *½ teaspoon ground cinnamon*
> *½ cup brown sugar, packed*
> *6 tablespoons (¾ stick) unsalted butter, cut up*
>
> *Sweetened whipped cream or vanilla ice cream*

* Use sliced or slivered almonds and chop by hand into slightly smaller pieces.

Preheat the oven to 350°. Peel, core, and slice the pears about ⅜ inch thick and place in a 9-by-12-inch baking pan (preferably Pyrex, or one you can use for serving). Sprinkle with the lemon juice. In a mixing bowl, combine the ingredients for the topping, mixing with your fingers until the mixture coheres and is crumbly. Scatter evenly over the pears. Bake, uncovered, for 20 to 25 minutes, or until the topping is lightly browned. Serve either warm or at room temperature with whipped cream or vanilla ice cream.

6 TO 8 SERVINGS

PECAN PIE

This recipe for pecan pie is less sweet than most. The sugar is reduced and brandy is added, which cuts the sweetness and contributes to the flavor in a subtle way.

FOR THE PIECRUST:

> *1½ cups flour*
> *3 tablespoons sugar*
> *⅛ teaspoon salt*
> *5 tablespoons unsalted butter, well chilled and cut into bits*
> *3 tablespoons vegetable shortening, well chilled*
> *Approximately ¼ cup cold water*

FOR THE FILLING:

> *3 eggs*
> *¼ cup plus 2 tablespoons sugar*
> *1 cup dark corn syrup**
> *1 teaspoon vanilla extract*
> *2 tablespoons brandy*
> *2 teaspoons cornstarch dissolved in 1 tablespoon cold water*
> *3 tablespoons unsalted butter, melted*
> *1½ cups pecan halves*

> *Sweetened whipped cream or vanilla ice cream*

* Do not substitute light corn syrup, which has less flavor and a cloying taste.

To make the piecrust: Combine the flour, sugar, and salt in a large mixing bowl. With the tips of your fingers, rub in the butter and shortening until broken down into small bits. Add just enough water to form a dough. (Or, using a food processor, make the piecrust according to the method on page 208.) Wrap the dough in wax paper and chill until firm enough to roll out (30 minutes or longer). Roll the dough into a circle between two lightly floured sheets of wax paper, and fit into a 9-inch pie plate, doubling and fluting the edges.

Preheat the oven to 350°.

To make the filling: Beat the eggs with an electric mixer, adding the sugar, corn syrup, vanilla, brandy, and cornstarch mixture. Stir in the melted butter and pecans and pour into the pie shell. Bake for 40 minutes, or just until the filling is set and the top crusty and slightly browned. Do not overcook or the pecans will darken and become bitter. Let cool on a wire rack and serve at room temperature with lightly sweetened whipped cream or vanilla ice cream.

6 TO 8 SERVINGS

Weighting a Piecrust

If you do not have dried beans or rice to weight the crust when prebaking it, try this method: First prick the bottom and sides of the shell with a fork. Then firmly press a sheet of aluminum foil inside the pan, completely covering the dough. This should be sufficient to keep the dough from sliding down the edges of the pan as it bakes. However, if you have another pie plate the same size, you can place it inside the pan you are using (over the foil) to weight the crust. (Note: If the piecrust is made with cream cheese or has an unusually high proportion of fat, it is best to weight it while baking.)

WARM PEAR-AMARETTO PIE

This is a luscious one-crust pie. The filling of pears in an amaretto-flavored custard is baked in a crust made with ground almonds. Although there are several steps to the recipe, it is quite easy to assemble.

FOR THE PIECRUST:

¾ cup slivered blanched almonds
1 cup flour
3 tablespoons sugar
Grated zest of 1 lemon
¼ pound (1 stick) unsalted butter, well chilled and
*   cut into bits*
1 egg yolk
2 tablespoons cold water, if necessary

FOR THE FILLING:

⅓ cup amaretto liqueur
2 tablespoons cornstarch
2 eggs
⅞ cup sugar
1 teaspoon vanilla extract
3 tablespoons unsalted butter, melted
3 medium-size or 4 small firm ripe Bartlett or Anjou
*   pears (1½ pounds)*

FOR THE TOPPING:

1 cup heavy cream
1 tablespoon amaretto liqueur
1 teaspoon vanilla extract
2½ teaspoons sugar

To make the piecrust: Preheat the oven to 350°. Spread the almonds in a pan and bake for 5 minutes, or just until faintly colored.
Grind in a food processor. Add the flour, sugar, and lemon zest and

blend. Add the butter and process briefly, turning the motor on and off, until the mixture resembles coarse meal. With the motor running, add the egg yolk and, if the mixture seems dry, a little water. Do not overprocess. Turn the mixture onto a sheet of wax paper before it coheres. Form the dough into a ball, cover with wax paper, and refrigerate until it is firm enough to roll out (30 minutes or longer).

Preheat the oven to 375°. Roll the dough between two sheets of lightly floured wax paper and fit into a 9-inch pie plate, doubling and fluting the edges. Line the shell with foil, fill with dry beans or rice, and bake for 18 minutes. Remove the foil and set the piecrust on a wire rack to cool thoroughly. Reduce the oven heat to 350°.

To make the filling: Mix the amaretto and cornstarch, stirring to dissolve. Lightly beat the eggs in a separate bowl and stir in the cornstarch mixture, the sugar, vanilla, and melted butter. Peel the pears, cut them in half lengthwise, and remove the stems and cores. Slice them crosswise ¼ inch thick, holding them in shape. Place each sliced pear half, cored side down, in the pie shell to form a radial design. Pour in the custard and bake for 45 to 55 minutes, or until the filling is set. If the crust starts to brown too much while baking, cover with a foil collar. Serve the pie warm.

To make the topping: Whip the cream lightly with the amaretto, vanilla, and sugar. Top each serving with a large spoonful of the whipped cream.

NOTE: If you are baking the pie ahead of time, let cool on a wire rack. To reheat, cover loosely with foil and place in a 325° oven for 10 to 15 minutes.

6 TO 8 SERVINGS

RASPBERRY-CASSIS FOOL

This is my favorite summer dessert, and it can be made in minutes. It is thought that the name derives from the French *fouler*, "to crush," although some argue that it is so named because any fool can make it.

3 pints red raspberries
3 tablespoons sugar
2 cups heavy cream
6 tablespoons cassis syrup

Rinse the raspberries very briefly and turn onto paper towels to dry. Put them in a bowl and toss with the sugar, slightly crushing a few of the berries. Let stand for 20 to 30 minutes.

Whip the cream with the cassis syrup until it holds firm peaks. Fold in the berries and any juice that has accumulated in the bowl. Do not overfold, as the mixture should be a bit streaky. Cover and chill until serving.

8 SERVINGS

SIMPLE FRESH-FRUIT DESSERTS

A bowl of fresh fruit is the simplest dessert of all, and often the most appealing. If you prefer, however, to serve the fruit with some sort of embellishment, consider the following easy preparations.

Berries Flavor strawberries, raspberries, or blackberries with a little sugar and curaçao or cassis syrup. Serve with shortbread or thin lemon cookies.

Oranges in Curaçao Cut the peel and all the white pith from seedless navel oranges and separate them into sections. Put in a bowl with a little curaçao, cover, and refrigerate until serving. (An attractive garnish can be made for this dessert by cutting the zest into slivers and simmering until transparent—about 20 minutes— in a syrup made from 1 cup sugar and ¾ cup water.)

Melon with Ginger Scatter minced preserved ginger stem over wedges of honeydew or cantaloupe and drizzle a little ginger syrup from the jar on top.

Fruit with Sour Cream Mix seedless green grapes or sliced peaches with sour cream sweetened to taste with brown sugar or honey.

Grapefruit and Mint Combine grapefruit sections with minced fresh mint leaves and sweeten with a little honey.

Fruit Salads   Combine two or more varieties of fruit, including some berries if they are available. If using melon, cut up and refrigerate separately so that the liquid can be drained off before serving. Add sugar to taste and, if desired, a liqueur flavoring such as kirsch or curaçao shortly before serving. Try peaches and raspberries with amaretto; or strawberries and orange sections with an orange liqueur; or a great variety of fruit, such as peaches, strawberries, blueberries, green grapes, oranges, and bananas, flavored with kirsch or Cointreau.

Sautéed Apples or Pears   In a heavy skillet, sauté peeled and sliced apples or pears for a few minutes or until tender in a little unsalted butter, adding sugar and ground cinnamon to taste. Sprinkle with brandy, applejack, or pear liqueur and serve warm with the juices from the pan and vanilla ice cream, if desired.

Baked Apples   Core, but do not peel, crisp, tart apples. Fill each cavity with a lump of butter, applejack, and sugar or with prepared mincemeat; put in a baking pan with a ½ inch of water, cover, and bake in a moderate oven for about ½ hour or until tender.

Pears in Wine   In a large saucepan, combine 2 cups dry red or white wine, 1 cup sugar, ½ cup water, a vanilla bean or a little vanilla extract, and a cinnamon stick. Put in 6 peeled pears and poach very gently until tender. Let cool in the syrup and serve chilled.

Baked Bananas   Peel bananas and slice in half lengthwise. Place cut side up in a buttered baking dish, dust lightly with ground cinnamon and brown sugar, and dot with unsalted butter. Bake in a 375° oven for 20 minutes. Heat a little curaçao or rum, pour over the bananas, ignite, and serve.

Sauce Romanoff   This is a traditional sauce for strawberries, but it goes well with other fresh fruits, such as cherries, peaches, blueberries, either alone or in combination. Whip 1 cup heavy cream with 2 tablespoons orange liqueur and, if desired, 1 tablespoon rum. Fold in 1 cup softened vanilla ice cream. (This makes about 1 pint, or enough for 6 to 8 servings of fruit.)

Do not add sweetener or liqueurs to a fruit salad until just before serving, as they tend to draw out the juices from the fruit, making the salad watery.

CAKES AND COOKIES

CHOCOLATE CURAÇAO CAKE

This is a very moist, chocolaty one-layer cake. It does not have a frosting (which would make it too rich), but is served with lightly whipped cream on the side.

8 ounces semisweet chocolate (not chocolate chips)
¼ pound (1 stick) unsalted butter
5 eggs, separated
⅔ cup sugar
2 tablespoons curaçao
1 teaspoon vanilla extract
⅓ cup ground pecans
1 tablespoon unsweetened cocoa

Confectioners' sugar

FOR THE TOPPING:

1 cup heavy cream
2 teaspoons sugar
½ teaspoon vanilla extract
1 tablespoon curaçao

Butter a round 9-inch cake pan. Cut a piece of wax paper to fit the bottom of the pan, and butter and flour the paper. Preheat the oven to 350°.

Break the chocolate into small pieces and melt it with the butter in the top of a double boiler over hot, not simmering, water, stirring constantly.

Beat the egg yolks until thick and light, gradually adding ⅓ cup of the sugar. Stir in the melted chocolate mixture along with the curaçao and vanilla.

Wash the beaters and beat the egg whites until they hold soft peaks. Continue beating until stiff as you gradually add the remaining sugar. Fold one-quarter of the beaten egg whites into the chocolate mixture. Sprinkle with the ground pecans and sift the cocoa over the top through a small strainer. Add the rest of the whites and fold everything together carefully but thoroughly. Turn into the prepared pan, spreading the batter evenly with a spatula. Bake for about 25 minutes. When done, the cake should be dry near the edges and moist in the center. Do not overcook or the cake will lose its creamy quality. Transfer to a wire rack and loosen the edges with a knife. Let cool in the pan for 20 minutes. Invert onto the rack, peel off the wax paper, and complete cooling. Turn onto a cake platter, bottom side up, as the top will have cracked slightly in cooling. Dust with confectioners' sugar just before serving.

Shortly before serving, lightly whip the cream with the sugar, vanilla, and curaçao. (Do not overbeat; it should be just stiff enough to mound slightly.) Serve the whipped cream in a bowl to be passed at the table.

8 SERVINGS

LEMON-GLAZED ALMOND CAKE

A moist one-layer cake with a syrup glaze.

*¼ pound (one stick)
 unsalted butter, softened
⅛ cup sugar
1 egg
¾ teaspoon almond extract
Grated zest of 2 lemons
1 cup flour*

*1½ teaspoons baking
 powder
⅔ cup slivered
 blanched almonds,
 ground
⅔ cup milk*

FOR THE GLAZE:

*3 tablespoons sugar
3 tablespoons lemon juice*

Preheat the oven to 325°. Cut a piece of wax paper to fit the bottom of a 9-inch round cake pan. Butter the paper and the sides of the pan.

With an electric mixer, cream the butter, adding the sugar gradually. Beat in the egg and the almond extract. Stir in the lemon zest. Sift the flour with the baking powder and combine with the ground almonds. Alternately add the flour mixture and the milk to the butter mixture, beginning and ending with flour. Turn into the prepared pan, spreading evenly. Bake for 30 to 35 minutes, or until a toothpick tests clean.

While the cake is baking, combine the sugar and lemon juice for the glaze in a small saucepan. Simmer gently for about 10 minutes, or until a light syrup forms.

When the cake is done, let cool for 5 minutes in the pan on a wire rack. Turn out onto the rack, peel off the wax paper, and carefully turn the cake over so that the top side is up. Spoon the warm syrup over the top of the cake and leave the cake on the rack to cool.

6 TO 8 SERVINGS

To Store Frosted or Glazed Cakes
If you do not have a cake dome, put toothpicks around the top of the cake to keep the plastic wrap from sticking to the icing.

STRAWBERRY CHARLOTTE

This is the fourth in a series of birthday cakes made for my husband. They have always been rich, multilayered constructions, very good, and not very easy to make. This one, however, was created in the spirit of simplicity, and, indeed, it can be made in about 15 minutes. It is, nevertheless, a worthy addition to the series.

2 pints strawberries
3 to 4 tablespoons sugar
3 tablespoons cassis syrup
2 cups heavy cream
2 teaspoons vanilla extract
Two 3-ounce packages ladyfingers

Rinse and hull the strawberries. Dry thoroughly on paper towels. Reserve a few berries for garnish. Slice the rest and mix in a bowl with 1½ tablespoons of the sugar and the cassis.

Whip the cream with the vanilla and 1½ to 2 tablespoons of the remaining sugar.

Line the bottom and sides of a 9-inch springform pan or an 8-cup soufflé dish with ladyfingers. Add half the berries, sprinkling with half the juice that has accumulated in the bowl. Cover with half the whipped cream. Add another layer of ladyfingers and then the remaining berries and juice. Spread the top of the cake with the rest of the cream. Cover with plastic wrap and chill for several hours before serving.

To serve: Garnish the top of the cake with the reserved strawberries. Remove the sides of the springform pan, or, if you are using a soufflé dish, serve the cake from the dish. Cut into wedges and lift out each piece with a large spoon and a flexible spatula.

6 SERVINGS

BLUEBERRY-LEMON CAKES

These are moist cake squares with a lemon-syrup glaze. They are good with afternoon tea or as an accompaniment to ice cream.

¼ pound (1 stick) unsalted butter, softened	1½ cups flour
	1½ teaspoons baking powder
1 cup sugar	¼ teaspoon salt
2 eggs	½ cup milk
Grated zest of 1 large lemon	1½ cups blueberries

FOR THE GLAZE:

¼ cup lemon juice
¼ cup sugar

Preheat the oven to 350°. Butter an 8- or 9-inch square baking pan.

Cream the butter with an electric mixer, adding the sugar gradually. Add the eggs and beat until light. Stir in the lemon zest. Sift together the flour, baking powder, and salt and add to the butter mixture alternately with the milk, beginning and ending with the flour. Fold in the blueberries. Spread evenly in the prepared pan and bake for about 35 minutes, or until a toothpick tests clean.

While the cake is baking, make the glaze: Mix the lemon juice and sugar in a small saucepan or stainless-steel measuring cup. Cook at a simmer for about 10 minutes, or until a light syrup forms. Spoon the syrup over the hot cake as soon as it is removed from the oven and let cool on a wire rack. To serve, cut into sixteen squares.

SIXTEEN 2-INCH SQUARES

CREAMY CHOCOLATE BROWNIES

The secret of these brownies is to undercook them. When cool, they will be custardlike inside and very chocolaty. The formula was developed by a family friend, Gertrud Blue.

3 squares Baker's unsweetened chocolate (3 ounces)
¼ pound (1 stick) unsalted butter
2 eggs
1 cup sugar
1 teaspoon vanilla extract
½ cup flour
Confectioners' sugar

Preheat the oven to 350°. Generously butter an 8-inch square baking pan. Melt the chocolate and butter, stirring constantly, in the top of a double boiler over hot, not simmering, water, or in a heavy saucepan over low heat. Reserve, allowing to cool.

With an electric mixer, beat the eggs until very thick and pale, adding the sugar gradually. Stir in the vanilla and melted-chocolate mixture. Fold in the flour, blending it in thoroughly. Turn into the prepared pan, and bake for 15 to 16 minutes. Do not be afraid to undercook the brownies—when done, a toothpick will test clean ½ inch from the edge of the pan; any further toward the center, the brownies should be moist. Let cool thoroughly in the pan on a wire rack, then place in the refrigerator for about 1 hour to firm before cutting. Cut into sixteen squares, transfer to a serving plate, and cover with plastic wrap. Dust with confectioners' sugar just before serving.

SIXTEEN 2-INCH BROWNIES

MARY CLAIRE'S OATMEAL COOKIES

These are delicious, thin, crisp cookies. They fill the house with a wonderful aroma while they are baking.

*½ pound (2 sticks)
unsalted butter,
softened
¾ cup granulated sugar
¾ cup brown sugar, packed
2 eggs
2 teaspoons vanilla extract
2 tablespoons milk*

*2 cups flour
1 teaspoon ground
cinnamon
½ teaspoon baking
soda
⅛ teaspoon salt
⅔ cup quick oats*

Preheat the oven to 350°. Lightly butter a large cookie sheet.

With an electric mixer, cream the butter with the granulated and brown sugars. Beat in the eggs, vanilla, and milk. Sift together the flour, cinnamon, baking soda, and salt and stir into the batter. When smooth, add the oats. Drop by half-teaspoonfuls 2 inches apart onto the cookie sheet. Bake for 8 minutes, or until very lightly browned. Let cool for a minute on the cookie sheet before transferring with a spatula to a wire rack.

5 TO 6 DOZEN

VEE'S SHORTBREAD

This recipe makes a fine, old-fashioned shortbread that has just the right firm and crisp texture. It keeps for several days in a tin in the cupboard or indefinitely in the freezer.

⅔ cup (11 tablespoons) unsalted butter
½ cup confectioners' sugar
1 to 2 tablespoons good quality vanilla extract
1½ cups plus 2 tablespoons flour

Preheat the oven to 325°. Butter a 9-inch square pan. Cream the butter with an electric mixer, gradually adding the sugar and the vanilla. Work in the flour with your hands or a fork. Pat evenly into the pan. Score with the tines of a fork in a grid pattern at 1-inch intervals. Bake for 35 to 40 minutes. The shortbread should not brown, but should be completely dry and cooked through. Let cool on a rack for 10 or 15 minutes and then cut into small squares when it is still slightly warm.

ABOUT 36 SMALL COOKIES

If you use a dark baking sheet when making cookies, watch them carefully. You will probably have to reduce the cooking time by a couple of minutes, as the cookies will brown faster than on a light-colored aluminum sheet.

ICE CREAMS
AND FROZEN DESSERTS

FROZEN CHOCOLATE GINGER MOUSSE

A creamy chocolate mousse punctuated with bits of preserved ginger stem.

> 4 squares (ounces) Baker's semisweet chocolate
> ½ cup plus 2 tablespoons heavy cream
> 1 tablespoon brandy
> 1 teaspoon vanilla extract
> 3 eggs, separated
> ¼ cup sugar
> 3 tablespoons preserved ginger stem, drained and diced

Cut the chocolate into small pieces and place in the top of a double boiler with 2 tablespoons of the cream. Melt over hot, not simmering, water, stirring constantly. Stir in the brandy and vanilla. Remove from the stove, but leave the chocolate over hot water.

Beat the egg yolks until thick and light. Stir in the melted chocolate. Set aside. Wash the beaters thoroughly and beat the egg whites until they hold firm peaks. Continue beating while gradually adding the sugar. Whip the remaining cream until it holds soft peaks. Fold the egg whites and cream into the chocolate mixture. Sprinkle the diced ginger on top and fold in. Turn into a serving bowl, cover with plastic wrap, and freeze until firm.

4 SERVINGS

GINGER ICE CREAM

This, like the Marrons Ice Cream that follows, has a very soft and creamy texture. It is flavored with bits of preserved ginger stem and a little brandy.

2 cups heavy cream
3 tablespoons brandy
3 tablespoons syrup from the preserved ginger stem
1 teaspoon vanilla extract
⅓ cup fine-diced preserved ginger stem
3 egg whites
⅔ cup sugar

Whip the cream with the brandy, syrup, and vanilla until it holds soft peaks. Fold in the ginger stem. Set aside. Wash the beaters thoroughly and beat the egg whites until they hold firm peaks. Continue beating while gradually adding the sugar. Fold the whites into the cream mixture. Turn into a serving bowl, cover with plastic wrap, and freeze until firm.

6 TO 8 SERVINGS

MARRONS ICE CREAM

The texture of this dessert is light and soft, the flavor delicious, and it is easy to make.

1 jar Raffetto marrons pieces
2 cups heavy cream
2½ tablespoons brandy
2 teaspoons vanilla extract
3 egg whites
¾ cup sugar

Put the marrons in a sieve, rinse briefly under running water to remove some of the syrup, and drain well.

Whip the cream with the brandy and vanilla until it holds soft peaks. Set aside. Wash the beaters thoroughly and beat the egg whites until almost stiff. Continue beating while gradually adding the sugar. With a rubber spatula, fold the whipped cream and egg whites together. Gently fold in the marrons. Turn into a serving bowl, cover tightly with plastic wrap, and freeze until firm.

6 TO 8 SERVINGS

Food will freeze faster in an empty freezer than in a full one. The temperature or freezing time should be adjusted accordingly when freezing ice cream, so that it will not be too firm.

MOCHA-ALMOND ICE CREAM

This is a splendid combination of flavors. The ice cream is smooth and creamy in texture, punctuated by specks of ground espresso and bits of chocolate.

4 egg whites
⅔ cup sugar
2 cups heavy cream
2 teaspoons vanilla extract
¾ teaspoon almond extract
2 teaspoons ground espresso (not instant)
1 tablespoon plus 1 teaspoon unsweetened cocoa, sifted
*1 square (ounce) Baker's semisweet chocolate, chopped
    fine*

Beat the egg whites until they hold firm peaks. Continue beating as you gradually add the sugar. In another bowl, whip the cream with the vanilla and almond extracts, the ground espresso, and the cocoa just until it holds soft peaks. Do not overbeat. Fold together the egg whites and cream. Fold in the chopped chocolate. Turn into a serving bowl, cover tightly with plastic wrap, and freeze until firm.

8 SERVINGS

ORANGE ICE CREAM

It is best to serve this ice cream soon after it has frozen or no later than the day after it has been made, as it will become hard if left in the freezer for too long.

1 envelope unflavored gelatin
¼ cup cold water
2 cups fresh orange juice (navel, temple, or Valencia)
2 cups heavy cream
½ cup sugar
⅓ cup curaçao

Soften the gelatin in the cold water and dissolve over low heat, stirring constantly. Remove from the heat and let stand while you proceed with the recipe.

Put the remaining ingredients in a bowl and beat with an electric mixer for 1 to 2 minutes to lighten the mixture. Continue beating while adding the dissolved gelatin in a thin stream. Turn into a serving bowl, cover tightly with plastic wrap, and place in the freezer until firm.

8 TO 10 SERVINGS

QUICK FRUIT ICE CREAMS

In making fruit-based ice creams over the past several years, I have found that cooking the fruit with sugar, rather than simply puréeing it, produces a smooth and soft ice cream without any icy bits of fruit and with a more intense flavor. Since I was, in fact, making a jam, it occurred to me that the same results could be achieved by substituting bottled jam or preserves for the fresh fruit and sugar in my recipes. This is a much quicker method, and you are not limited to fruits in season. Recipes follow for black cherry, peach, raspberry, and strawberry ice creams. Using this method you can, of course, experiment with other fruit preserves. Be sure to use a good-quality commercially prepared jam that is not too stiff or too sweet (or better still, homemade preserves, if you have them). The proportions may have to be altered slightly in each recipe, depending on the jam you are using, as some brands will be sweeter than others. In calling these "quick" ice creams, I refer to the time invested by the cook; once they are put into your freezer, they will require the usual 4 to 6 hours to become firm.

QUICK BLACK CHERRY ICE CREAM

Black cherry preserves are not easy to find, except in specialty stores. If you are successful in locating a jar, this ice cream is well worth trying. Two excellent brands are imported from Switzerland: Hero and Fischlin. If you use the latter, which contains kirsch, do not add the kirsch called for in the recipe.

> *2 cups heavy cream*
> *⅔ cup Hero or ¾ cup Fischlin black cherry preserves*
> *2½ tablespoons kirsch (optional)*

Using an electric mixer, whip the cream with the preserves and kirsch, if you are using it, until the mixture holds soft peaks. Turn into a serving bowl, cover with plastic wrap, and freeze until firm.

APPROXIMATELY I QUART

QUICK PEACH ICE CREAM

> *2 cups heavy cream*
> *1 cup peach preserves or jam (such as Smucker's)*
> *2 to 3 tablespoons brandy*

Using an electric mixer, whip the cream and the peach jam until the mixture holds soft peaks. Fold in the brandy, according to taste. Turn into a serving bowl, cover with plastic wrap, and freeze until firm.

APPROXIMATELY I QUART

QUICK RASPBERRY ICE CREAM

This ice cream has a pure, fresh raspberry flavor and is best without the addition of any liqueur. Seedless blackberry preserves may be substituted for the raspberry.

2 cups heavy cream
¾ cup seedless red raspberry preserves (preferably
  Trappist brand)

Using an electric mixer, whip the cream with the raspberry preserves until the mixture holds soft peaks. Turn into a serving bowl, cover with plastic wrap, and freeze until firm. Remove from the freezer and let stand at room temperature for 15 to 30 minutes before serving.

APPROXIMATELY 1 QUART

QUICK STRAWBERRY ICE CREAM

2 cups heavy cream
¾ cup plus 1 tablespoon strawberry jam or preserves
2 tablespoons curaçao (optional)

Using an electric mixer, whip the cream with the jam and curaçao until the mixture holds soft peaks. Turn into a serving bowl, cover with plastic wrap, and freeze until firm.

APPROXIMATELY 1 QUART

WAYS OF SERVING
STORE-BOUGHT ICE CREAM

For those occasions when you would like to serve a homemade dessert but have run out of time, the following suggestions may prove useful.

With Ginger and Chocolate Dice preserved or crystallized ginger stem and fold into softened vanilla ice cream with, if desired, a little brandy. Serve the ice cream with warmed chocolate sauce on top.

Coupe Aux Marrons Top each serving of vanilla ice cream with a large spoonful of marrons pieces* mixed with a little brandy.

With Applesauce Heat applesauce, flavor it with ground cinnamon, and serve over vanilla or butter pecan ice cream.

With Amaretto Stir amaretto liqueur into softened coffee ice cream. Crumble amaretti cookies (hard Italian macaroons) and swirl through the ice cream or sprinkle on top.

Cassis-Strawberry Stir a little cassis syrup into softened vanilla ice cream and swirl strawberry preserves through the mixture.

Butterscotch-Coffee Serve coffee ice cream with a topping of warm butterscotch sauce.

* Available in jars in gourmet sections of supermarkets. Raffetto is a widely distributed brand.

Mocha Pour a little chocolate-flavored liqueur, such as crème de cacao, over coffee ice cream; or serve chocolate ice cream with a coffee liqueur, such as Tía María.

Peach Swirl peach preserves through softened vanilla ice cream, adding, if you like, a little brandy. Or serve peach ice cream with a topping of sliced fresh peaches.

Blueberry Swirl blueberry preserves through softened lemon or vanilla ice cream; or top the ice cream with fresh blueberries.

With Strawberries or Oranges Serve lemon or orange sherbet or vanilla ice cream with a topping of fresh strawberries or navel orange sections macerated in curaçao.

Maple-Pecan Serve vanilla ice cream with a topping of warm maple syrup mixed with toasted, chopped pecans.

An open bottle of maple syrup is likely to spoil if it is not kept in the refrigerator.

Coconut Pulverize unsweetened coconut in a food processor and stir into softened vanilla ice cream with, if desired, a little amaretto liqueur.

Peanut Mix crumbled peanut brittle into softened vanilla ice cream.

Cappuccino   Stir a little ground cinnamon and sifted cocoa into softened coffee ice cream and grate semisweet baking chocolate on top.

Index

Basil (continued)
    sautéed cherry tomatoes with, 165
    storing, 11
    tip on chopping, 10
    tortellini with fresh, 19
    vichyssoise with fresh, 10
Bean(s):
    green, 159
    salad, white, 180
    soup, black, 31
Beef:
    cold fillet with caper-mustard
        sauce, 141
    Delmonico steaks with mushroom
        and peppercorn sauce, 71
    short ribs with barbecue sauce, 90
    steak salad, 137
    steak tartare Casanova, 140
    stew
        with apples and ginger, 27
        with orange and cumin, 29
    to cook rare, 142
Beets, baked, 154
Berries, 222
Biscuits:
    blueberry drop, 186
    buttermilk, 187
Black:
    bean soup, 31
    cherry ice cream, 240
    olives and cream, pasta with, 119
Blueberry:
    cobbler, 206
    drop biscuits, 186
    lemon cakes, 230
    with ice cream, 243
Boiled lobster, 97
Bread:
    bacon-corn, 184
    baguettes with melted Brie, 198
    blueberry drop biscuits, 186
    buttermilk biscuits, 187
    corn muffins, 189
    easy
        cheddar, 189
        sour cream, 192

Bread (continued)
    herb and Parmesan, 198
    Italian, with roast peppers, mush-
        rooms, and olives, 199
    Middle Eastern, 200
    miniature lime muffins, 193
    open-face cucumber sandwiches,
        201
    popovers, 194
    quick walnut, 195
    scones, 196
    tip on, 188
    yeast, about, 191
Brie, melted:
    baguettes with, 198
    canapés, 21
Broccoli, 154
Broilers, lemon, with basil, 80
Brook trout with dill and caper sauce,
    97
Brownies, creamy chocolate, 231
Buttered cabbage, 155
Butterflied leg of lamb, 59
Buttermilk biscuits, 187
Butterscotch-coffee ice cream, 242

Cabbage:
    buttered, 155
    soup, potato, leek, and, 51
Cake(s):
    blueberry-lemon, 230
    chocolate-curaçao, 225
    lemon-glazed almond, 227
    strawberry charlotte, 229
    tip on, 188
    to store frosted or glazed, 228
Cantaloupe, sliced avocado and, 175
Caper:
    mustard sauce, cold beef fillet
        with, 141
    sauce, brook trout with dill and,
        97
    vinaigrette, avocados with, 14
Cappuccino, flavoring for ice cream,
    244

Shellfish. See Fish and Shellfish
Short ribs with barbecue sauce, 90
Shortbread, Vee's, 233
Shrimp and avocado, 23
Simple fresh-fruit desserts, 222–224
Sliced avocado and cantaloupe, 175
Soft-shell crabs, sautéed, 104
Sole and scallop ragout, 106
Sorrel, endive, and chive salad, 171
Soufflé, cheese, 114
Soup:
    black bean, 31
    chilled
        carrot and peach, 3
        cucumber and honeydew, 4
        spinach and mint, 6
    cioppino, 37
    cream of artichoke, 7
    fish
        chowder, 39
        gumbo, 40
    fisherman's stew, 43
    minestrone, 45
    onion and mushroom, 48
    potato, leek, and cabbage, 51
    sauerkraut, pork, and mushroom,
        53
    scallop, tomato, and tortellini, 54
    tomato, orange, and fennel, 8
    tortellini in brodo, 9
    vichyssoise with fresh basil, 10
Sour cream:
    bread, easy, 192
    chive sauce, 168
    fruit with, 222
Spareribs:
    choucroute garnie, 68
    Lee Jones's, with barbecue sauce,
        77
Spinach:
    and mint soup, chilled, 6
    avocado, and red pepper salad,
        176
    creamed, 156
    sauce, pasta with, 120
    tip on cooking, 7

Steak(s):
    Delmonico, with mushroom and
        peppercorn sauce, 71
    salad, 137
    tartare Casanova, 149
Steamed mussels, 109
Stew:
    beef
        with apples and ginger, 27
        with orange and cumin, 29
    chili, 34
    fisherman's, 43
    veal shanks braised with arti-
        chokes, 92
Store-bought ice cream, ways to serve,
    242–244
Strawberry(ies):
    cassis ice cream, 242
    charlotte, 229
    ice cream, quick, 241
    ice cream with, 243
Swordfish:
    in an Italian marinade, 110
    with lime, mint, and tarragon
        sauce, 113

Tarragon:
    cold roast chicken with lime and,
        144
    sauce, swordfish with lime, mint,
        and, 113
Thyme, fresh, and lemon, game hens
    with, 73
Tiny peas and sugar snap peas, 161
Tomato(es):
    and fresh herbs, rice salad with,
        174
    and mozzarella, pasta with, 120
    aspic with sour-cream-chive sauce,
        166
    cherry
        canapés, 21
        sautéed, with basil, 165
        with cottage cheese, 21
    note on, xvi
    orange, and fennel soup, 8

For many years Helen Hecht lived in New York City, where she pursued a career in book publishing. She now resides in Washington, D.C., where her husband, Anthony Hecht, is professor of English at Georgetown University and their son, Evan, is in the eighth grade. Mrs. Hecht is also the author of Cuisine for All Seasons, Cold Cuisine: Summer Food to Prepare in Advance and Serve at Leisure *and co-author of* Gifts in Good Taste. *Her food articles have appeared in* Vogue *and* Cuisine *magazines.*